# What others are saying about Conviction Marketing

*"Listen to Kelly. She is an inspiring, unstoppable force."*
~ Kara Goldin, Founder & CEO of Hint, Inc. and WSJ Best Selling Author of Undaunted

*"If you're a thought leader looking to go straight to the top—and be the best in what you do—you need Kelly and her guide to a conviction-based brand. To be the most valuable person in the room, you want to build a brand that authentically aligns with who you are and what you believe. Kelly shows you the way."*
~ Bo Eason, NFL All-Pro, In-Demand Speaker & 7-Time Best-Selling Author

*"Kelly has written a compelling book on what it takes to become a true thought leader, by leading with conviction when many find it easier to conform."*
~ David Meltzer, Co-founder of Sports 1 Marketing Agency

*"Kelly Roach has written a must-read for any entrepreneur looking to stand out from the crowd while remaining firm to their conviction."*
~Ken Coleman, #1 national bestselling author of The Proximity Principle and nationally syndicated host of The Ken Coleman Show.

*"Kelly is one of the most brilliant and generous leaders I know. When it comes to building your business, finding the confidence to put yourself out there, stepping into your next level, and doing it all with such*

*authenticity and integrity - she is your ultimate go-to! As she always says, "We zig when they zag" and no one does it better than Kelly."*

~ Cathy Heller, host of iTunes #1 podcast
Don't Keep Your Day Job

*"It's rare I meet a female leader that is so REAL as Kelly! She's smart and when most people hit a hard moment in life they pull back and allow their emotions to stop them. Kelly prepares for a "Rainy Day" and set's her business up to succeed in any market. Read her book with a highlighter. It's brilliant!"*

~ Shanda Sumpter, founder and
Queen Visionary of HeartCore Business

*"Nothing excites me more than watching women unapologetically blaze trails, clear paths and lift other women up in their pursuit of a meaningful business and life. Kelly Roach is a shining example of this! She's a whip-smart, generous leader who serves from the heart and dishes out no-nonsense business advice that, when implemented, can make you millions. This book is a taste of the impact she can have in your life and is the closest thing you can get to picking her brain for less than your weekly latte spends."*

~ Jill Stanton, Co-Founder,
Wealthy Course Creator

# Conviction Marketing

A guide to authority, influence,
and market leadership online

**By Kelly Roach**

*Business Educator and Leadership Strategist*

*Conviction Marketing*
*A guide to authority, influence, and industry leadership online*

Independently published

Copyright © 2022

All rights reserved. No part of this book may be reproduced, stored in a retrieval system, or transmitted in any form or by any means without the written permission of the publisher.
Printed in the United States of America.

ISBN: 979-8-9854806-0-3

Cover design by Sean Foran

DISCLAIMER AND/OR LEGAL NOTICES
While the publisher and authors have used their best efforts in preparing this book, they make no representations or warranties with respect to the accuracy or completeness of the contents of this book. The advice and strategies contained herein may not be suitable for your situation. You should consult a professional where appropriate. Neither the publisher nor the authors shall be liable for any loss of profit or any other commercial damages, including but not limited to special, incidental, consequential, or other damages. The purchaser or reader of this publication assumes responsibility for the use of these materials and information. Adherence to all applicable laws and regulations, both advertising and all other aspects of doing business in the United States or any other jurisdiction, is the sole responsibility of the purchaser or reader.

*This book is intended to provide accurate information with regard to the subject matter covered. However, the Author and the Publisher accept no responsibility for inaccuracies or omissions, and the Author and Publisher specifically disclaim any liability, loss, or risk, whether personal, financial, or otherwise, that is incurred as a consequence, directly or indirectly, from the use and/or application of any of the contents of this book.*

# Dedication

To Billy and Madison:
you are the magic and miracles in my life.

# Table of Contents

Introduction                                                          1

Chapter One: - Conviction Marketing vs. the "Copy/Paste"
Trap                                                                  6

Chapter Two: - The Conviction Marketing Pyramid        19

Chapter Three: - Identifying Your Differentiating Beliefs 47

Chapter Four: - Creating Messaging that Matters         62

Chapter Five: - Turn Your Convictions into a Tribe
Mentality                                                            79

Chapter Six: - The Fortune Is in the Follow-Through    92

Chapter Seven: - Revolt Against the Norms                  102

Chapter Eight: - 5 Essential Steps to Catapult Your
Business to a Category of One                                  108

Chapter Nine: - Your Moral Compass Makes Your
Marketing Matter                                                   114

Chapter Ten: - The Millionaire Visionary                    124

About the Author                                                   132

# Introduction

Your superpower is a combination of the dreams you hold inside of you and the unique talents you have been gifted with to make them a reality.

When we start on the path of entrepreneurship, we KNOW there is a better way; we believe we can make a difference, and we commit to working to do so until we make our little dent in the world. We have stars in our eyes and butterflies in our stomach as we embark on the entrepreneurial journey, envisioning the life we will create and the income and impact we will make… and then we get hit over the head with a ton of bricks. This is HARD.

Entrepreneurship is not for the faint of heart. It tests every fiber of our being; it cracks us open and reveals every weakness, every mindset block, every trauma still stored inside of us. In this pursuit of bringing our gifts to the world each day, we are faced with a new set of challenges that screams in our faces, "HOW BAD DO YOU WANT IT?" In each and every moment, we must return to our why, remember what drove us to get started in the first place, and find the will and desire to push to the next phase.

I've gone through this labyrinth with four of my own companies and have helped thousands of entrepreneurs "find their way" online so they could:

- Achieve financial and time freedom
- Put their family first
- Create a business that authentically represents who they are and the difference they want to make in the world

I have had the privilege and opportunity of identifying the pitfalls and traps that destroy businesses as well as the distinct and specific strategies that catapult, differentiate, and elevate brands to world-class status.

It is fascinating to watch the same pattern repeat itself over and over again, in which millions of entrepreneurs strike out on their own with huge goals, a hunger to change the world, and a quest to claim their destiny, only to end up broke, burned out, and in debt vs. financially free. This is a preventable phenomenon, and this book is aimed at helping you intelligently chart your own course so you can fast forward to the moment in time where you look around and say "I made it."

The truth is that growing a business is the greatest personal development exercise of all time, which I am sure you have heard many times before. The reason this is such a critical thing to understand is because your business will never grow beyond you. As entrepreneurs and leaders, we need to recognize that our business grows *from* us and *through* us, and it is only in our ability to stretch beyond our past that we can create a more compelling future.

Most entrepreneurs get so fearful in their marketing and their approach to growing their business that they only look to "proven" topics, tactics, and talk points.

They put themselves in a fixed box of mediocrity because they are made to feel that, if they just follow this template, say these magic words, teach this thing the same way everyone else does, raving fans will automatically arrive. There is so much pressure in building a business that we sometimes hedge our bets doing what feels safe at the cost of doing what truly lights us up, avoiding the deep work we are actually being called to do.

What is important to understand is that there are layers to the psychology of buying, and there is a place for tactics. However, it's incredibly important that you intentionally move into your message. I am writing this book to help you understand how to effectively articulate your million-dollar idea—one that is unique to you—while using proven, profitable strategies that allow you to create raving fans who turn into dream clients over and over again, with no limit to what you can achieve. Social media marketing is an abundant playground of 24/7 opportunity if you know how to leverage it. I can't wait to show you how.

Leading up to writing this book, I learned a very important lesson about leading with conviction that I want to share with you here in the hopes that it will inspire you to do the same.

Back when I was getting started online, I played in the little box that we all do from time to time. I took the courses, followed the proven methods, and did exactly what I was told.

When I was ready to do my first product launch, I did what most entrepreneurs do—I found the most well-known launch teacher and followed their method to a T. I did that over and over again, each time getting more worn down, more exhausted, and more skeptical of the fact that this could, or would, *ever* work for me. After several rounds of losing money on launches, I began looking at what I was doing and questioning if this was the best way. My conclusion? It wasn't. I realized this was going to have to be a stake-in-the-ground moment for me and for the rest of the entrepreneurs out there struggling to launch their offers, because as Einstein said, the definition of insanity is doing the same thing over and over again expecting a different result. It was time for me to stop the insanity.

I ripped apart everything we had been doing and rebuilt it *my way*, based on what I knew would work for me. I listened to my intuition and natural instincts. A few hundred revisions later, we had created *The Live Launch Method*. At first, we were a tiny minnow in a huge ocean, swimming with sharks and whales. But, after a few years and teaching over 40,000 people the *Live Launch* difference, the method is now accepted as THE most effective way to launch online.

The Live Launch took us from a 7-figure company to multiple 8-figures, and now it will carry us to 9-. Sit with that for a moment. Having the courage to stand in your convictions could be the thing that takes you from unknown to undisputed leader, making millions of dollars and changing countless lives in the process.

When we first went to market with our message, it was the exact opposite of the widely-accepted methodology being taught by industry giants. It was risky, and it was not instantly rewarded. However, as we continued to press forward and demonstrate through our results and our clients' results, it became undeniable that the method was superior. Fast forward to today, and the very giants we were up against are now using and promoting their own version of The Live Launch.

Moral of the story: YOU HAVE THE POWER TO CHANGE THE WORLD. If you can quiet your mind, open your heart, and get strategically aligned in your approach, you might just surprise yourself and those around you with the massive difference you can make. Let me show you how!

# Chapter One:

# Conviction Marketing vs. the "Copy/Paste" Trap

*"In order to be irreplaceable, one must always be different."*

**-Coco Chanel**

The online business world is changing faster than we can fathom. While the opportunities are endless, we have to stop, listen, and pay attention to what our customer wants, needs, and demands from us in order to capitalize on the opportunity in the next evolution ahead. As their needs and desires constantly change, it's imperative that you remain on the frontlines of those changes in the online world when it comes to marketing. However, the secret to cutting through the noise isn't another flashy tactic or new platform; it's the ability to create an entirely new lane in your industry. It's kicking the status quo and leveraging something only *you* have—your convictions.

*The Conviction Marketing Method* is not just a new shiny object in the online marketing world. It is the key to becoming a category of one, the uncontested leader in your industry. It's how you separate yourself from the rest of your industry and move from "online influencer" mode and into the role of industry icon.

What used to captivate large audiences is now met with skepticism as the online world is getting more and more sophisticated. Gone are the days of perfectly curated Instagram feeds and 300-step funnels with overly-edited videos.

Thankfully, smart people are 100 percent *over it,* and they are ready, waiting, and seeking leadership from people who are courageously willing to lead with vision. People just like you!

We are entering into a brand new season of online marketing that celebrates authenticity, courage, and real leadership. It's become clear that so many of those self-proclaimed gurus actually have very little to offer in the way of real transformation and thought leadership. If you've ever felt like you didn't fit into the cookie-cutter mold of the online world, then you are in the right place.

The principles in this book will teach you a revolutionary approach to building an audience full of raving fans and walk you through what it looks like to launch industry-changing movements by enrolling people in your vision and bringing them on board to disrupt the status quo. The main ingredient to this game-changing approach? Conviction.

## What is Conviction?

Merriam-Webster defines conviction as: *a strong persuasion or belief.* Those who dare to carve out their own path and allow their beliefs to drive their marketing will ultimately win.

In a world full of gurus touting the newest, hottest trends, there are legions of entrepreneurs following their every recommendation and mimicking everything they do. Unfortunately, when you are simply copying someone else's marketing strategies, using templates, hopping on every trend, using their stock photos, and filling in the blanks on captions used by thousands of people, you are all simply solidifying your place as a second-rate version of someone else. But it doesn't have to be that way. You are your own competitive edge. You, your experience, and your convictions are what set you apart from everyone else in your industry. While it might be tempting to simply replicate what others are doing (that seems to be working), that won't catapult you into becoming an industry thought leader. Only your convictions can do that.

> *An unwillingness to settle for the status quo is what sets the ultra successful apart.*

Conviction is the foundation on which my company was built. It's what took us from 6- to 7- to 8-figures, and it's what's catapulted our brand into the industry leader we've become. Conviction is what compelled me to create a year-long program in a set of 6-week courses. It's what drove our decision to build our programs with a high level of human connection and support in a world that is obsessed with automation. It's what led to the creation of the most powerful launch method on the planet, creating 6- and 7-figure leaps for both our company and our clients' companies. And I believe it can do the same for you.

## Don't Settle

An unwillingness to settle for the status quo is what sets the ultra-successful apart from the online copycat world. Conviction marketing, at its core, is building your go-to market strategy on the foundational principles that drive you. It's leaning into what you believe is right, even if that is the opposite of what the rest of your industry is doing. It's leading with courage when others aren't willing to do the same, and it's speaking the heart language of your people, who are desperately waiting for your message. Only those who understand the power, necessity, and positioning of their convictions will thrive and survive this next evolution in the online world.

As a business strategist for the past 10 years, I get asked the same questions over and over again. At the top of almost everyone's list is some version of the question: "How do I stand out in a crowded market and attract high-ticket clients who want and can afford my offers?" The answer is always: by leaning into what makes you entirely different from the rest of your industry. It's zigging when everyone else zags. It's finding and filling the gaps in your market, because you believe your people deserve better! It's not using a plug-and-play method that thousands of others are using.

For each of you reading this book, you know that something different is required to elevate your brand and enable you to stand out. You are being called to create a pattern interrupt for your market, to disrupt the expected, and to lead in a way that inspires the rest of your industry to follow.

The truth is that market saturation is at an all-time high, and it will only continue to increase as more and more people enter the online space. The barrier to entry is zero. In 30 seconds or less, anyone can go into business, post a picture that looks like yours, a bio that mirrors yours, and take your years of impact and true thought leadership and claim it as their own. It happens every day.

In this post-pandemic era, traditional business owners have learned the critical nature of building an online presence. The floodgates have opened, and millions of businesses that previously relied on walk-in traffic are now seeking a way to survive by selling online. The overcrowding and explosion of competition will continue to climb, BUT when you refuse to follow the crowd and decide to allow your convictions and your results to speak for themselves, you will prevail regardless of the noise.

In the pages of this book, I will outline how I disrupted my industry, the pitfalls I faced along the way, the hundreds of successful clients who have followed my lead to generate millions of dollars in their markets, and the compelling reasons to infuse more conviction into your marketing efforts. By the end of this book, you will be fired up and ready to step forward as a movement maker and true peerless leader in your industry.

If you feel an internal calling to bring forth a new set of ideas, but you're holding back because you're worried about stepping into new territory, this book is for you. I'm writing this book to help real experts like you disrupt themselves and their markets with integrity, innovation, and an undeniably unstoppable spirit.

This one is for the rebels. The trailblazers. The leaders with courage, willing to lean into their convictions, and stand up for what they believe is right.

Now is your moment to step into your next level of thought leadership, and in the following pages, I am going to give you a roadmap to cultivating your legacy work.

This book isn't for those who aren't true experts, who don't get transformational results, and who are happy to blend in with the crowd. It's not for those looking for the path of least resistance, or those unwilling to stand up for what they believe.

It's time to stand out among the sea of competition and find your blue ocean. It's time to claim your role as an industry leader.

## The Online Marketing Dilemma

When I first started my business, we didn't have live streaming; there were FAR fewer social media apps available, and informational content was 100% king. However, over the last 10 years, the volume of information has multiplied exponentially by the minute, meaning that you need far more in today's online world than a mountain of how-to content.

The market is now so saturated with instructional content that consumers no longer value educational materials the way they once did. And, coupled with that, they have to do so much sorting to find a new idea or useful piece of information because of the low-quality, high-volume approach so many have taken in the way they build their businesses online.

When I was ready to scale my business and start selling to dozens, if not hundreds, of people at a time vs. 1 to 1, I was overwhelmed by all the information on launching. I bought all the courses, did everything the gurus told me, and nothing was working. The information was plentiful, but the results were non-existent. There was a huge disconnect between all that I was reading and learning, and what actually worked in this ever-changing online world. And it wasn't just me. My market was experiencing the same thing. The clients and customers I most wanted to reach had decision fatigue and were overwhelmed with the barrage of information being constantly thrown at them. As a result, my revenue suffered and so did my impact, despite my significant business experience and success in my former career as a Senior Vice President of Sales at a Fortune 500.

I have learned over the last few years the importance of having the courage to create a totally new conversation with your market. I have learned through personal experience that millions and millions of dollars of income will come to those who have the foresight and forward-thinking mentality to avoid jumping on the bandwagon of "copy/paste" marketing, and instead have the patience, the long-term vision, and commitment to create a conversation with the market that no one has ever before initiated. This is Conviction Marketing.

Conviction marketing is all about straying away from the conversation currently happening in your market and creating a completely new one instead.

Few business owners will be willing to utilize this strategy, because they are scared of stepping out of line and missing out on the small quick wins. They settle for pennies now, instead of doing the work to build a brand that generates millions.

Throughout this book, I am going to give you a myriad of strategies to help you understand not only how to live and lead with conviction, but also how to differentiate everything about your brand and your positioning so that you truly become the one and only in your space.

This process and journey will require introspection. It will require quieting down. It will require you digging deep in your heart and in your mind to align with your soul purpose in a way that maybe you haven't ever done before—or haven't done in years.

I want to help you understand the difference between empty opinions/platitudes and convictions. I want to help you understand how to leverage how-to content, how to layer on hope, and how to not only speak your convictions, but back them up with strength and real results.

## What Conviction Marketing is NOT

Conviction marketing is about leading with what you stand *for*, not merely what you stand *against*. Many business owners post negative or derogatory feedback, opinions, or thoughts about what is happening in their space or what their competitors are doing. These are empty ideas and scarcity-minded platitudes that do nothing but perpetuate negativity and get a few comments.

This is the furthest thing from conviction marketing, which is truly about pioneering a new path. It's innovation and out-performing your competitors. It's committing to doing the work to show your market that you don't just espouse empty complaints, but that you lead with vision and have the proof to back it up.

Sharing ideas, opinions, and platitudes is easy. Making an off-the-cuff statement because you are trying to tear someone down and, in turn, lift yourself up is the norm in online marketing today. Instead, I want you to commit to identifying all of the frustration, anger, and upset your ideal clients face, and actually *do something about it*.

Conviction marketing comes down to you identifying the strong, underlying beliefs you possess about the world you work in and what your ideal clients truly deserve, and translating those things very specifically into:

- A program, service, or offer that meets the needs not currently being addressed correctly by the mass market in your space.

- A clear message around what's missing in your market and how YOU are stepping in to provide that. This includes a content marketing strategy built around these convictions that positions you in a class of your own, with three key layers: how-to content, hope content, and conviction content.

- A go-to-market strategy you repeatedly deliver that builds your brand, communicates your distinct difference, and allows people to engage with you and your transformative work prior to ever handing over a dime.

For years, the same messages have been regurgitated across industries. I like to call this "copy/paste" marketing in which so many business owners feel safer offering the same thing their competitors do for fear that they will miss out if they are not "competitive."

This worked when the market was less saturated, but today you have to be different. Waving your hand and saying "me too" is not enough. Offering the same solution as your competition with a different name and graphic attached to it will no longer do the job.

You need to learn how to listen to your intuition, draw your own conclusions, and utilize your own life experiences and ideas to bring something new to market, so your people are better served, and have access to a better process that gets them better results.

## What Will You Do With It?

It's worth noting the fact that we have extremely limited time on this planet, and nothing is promised to us, not even tomorrow. I know that you started your business with a deep desire and calling to do something *real*. But it is easy along the way to forget your why and start going along to get along.

Throughout the course of this book, I want you to look inward and allow your deepest, truest feelings and desires to come forward.

Many times, we shut down and become removed from the desires that once fueled us when we first started in business. Life gets crazy, and things get hard, and in the midst of the chaos, we don't feel as though we have the energy to truly allow our convictions to lead us. We worry what people will think. We question whether we can really rise to the occasion. We allow the gurus to shove us in a box and tell us the only way to truly embrace success is to do it *their* way. But that couldn't be further from the truth.

I want to reverse your thinking on this to help you realize that leading with your convictions and putting that stake in the ground that you stand for something is *everything.* Standing for what your market deserves, standing for what they actually *need*, and being willing to take the bold brave action to do everything you can to fulfill these desperately missing and lacking pieces of the puzzle is everything.

So open your heart and your mind as we progress into the next chapter where we will help you identify and understand your differentiating beliefs and step into your power to bring them forward in the market.

## Establishing Your Convictions

- Your market is craving new and next-level leadership. They are ready for thought leaders like you.

- Create a pattern interrupt to cut through the current noise and clutter.

- Zero cost of entry has led to an overabundance of copycat business owners. Don't be one of them.

- Conviction marketing is about creating an entirely new conversation, one that delivers value and results.

- It is easy to share opinions about what is wrong in any industry. What your prospects want are solutions.

- Conviction marketing is hard work, but it is the only way to differentiate yourself in order to boost your business and bank account.

# Chapter Two:

# The Conviction Marketing Pyramid

*"In a crowded marketplace, fitting in is a failure. In a busy marketplace, not standing out is the same as being invisible."*

**-Seth Godin**

I t is very interesting to be a participant, teacher, and consumer—all at once—in the online marketing space. It's fascinating really. You watch the same trends, traps, and cycles over and over again.

I see so many entrepreneurs spend all their time chasing tactics as their "go-to-market" strategy. "How to build your email list," "how to go viral on TikTok," or whatever the new shiny object might be. And what I will say about this is YES, that *will* work, but not for long, and it's only one small piece of a very large marketing puzzle.

Tactic-based marketing centered on the "trends" or misconceptions of unknowing consumers will absolutely get you engagement and quick, short-term results from those looking for a solution. But focusing solely on that level of marketing makes you a commodity. It is transactional at best and will quickly cause you to become irrelevant if you never layer on anything other than simple, informational content.

## The Magic Marketing Formula

The most common mistake entrepreneurs make when it comes to marketing online is going to market with a one-dimensional, informational approach.

While how-to content is a critical piece of the marketing puzzle, most never move beyond that to a more sophisticated model. They stay stuck in a constant struggle to chase the latest, greatest trends, never fully embracing their own unique competitive edge.

For the last 10 years, my team and I have used what I am about to teach you as our foundational go-to-market strategy. It's what propelled us into a category of one in our very saturated industry and brought us to 8 figures as a company, quickly on our way to 9.

But, before I dive into our model, I want to be clear: there is no one-size-fits-all approach to marketing online. In fact, that's the entire point of this book. The Conviction Marketing Method is a lens through which I want you to look at your marketing. It is about identifying what makes you wildly unique and marketing in a way that carves out a new path for those in your industry. It isn't a posting schedule.

There are no templates. Every person reading this book will apply this strategy differently. But that's the point.

What this model does is it allows you to think critically about how you are building your brand and carving out your legacy. It is meant to propel you from influencer to industry icon and set you apart from the rest of your market, no matter how crowded.

This method is for those who are brave enough to say good-bye to copy-paste strategies that keep you stuck. It's for those who know and understand that, by embracing your beliefs and convictions, you are actually able to show up and serve your market in a way that will be completely unmatched by your peers.

This isn't a here today, gone tomorrow approach; it's how you blaze new trails and solidify your spot as both thought leader and category of one in your industry.

> *By embracing your beliefs and convictions, you are actually able to show up and serve your market in a way that will be completely unmatched by your peers.*

In our business education companies, we work with hundreds of clients in countless different industries across the globe. This framework is what has allowed each of them to claim the "go-to" spot in their market, because it helps them to stand out, command attention, build authority, gain trust, and create absolute buy-in from their followers. It has led to millions of dollars earned by everyday people with extraordinary vision willing to do the work and lead.

Even during a global pandemic, our clients were able to make massive leap after massive leap in their businesses, because they stood up with conviction and created a space for ideal clients who wanted and deserved more.

## The Pyramid

The Conviction Marketing Method is built on the idea of a content-style pyramid. Each layer of the pyramid is important, and they all play a different role in your go-to-market strategy.

Depending on what season of business you are in, you may use more of one than the other. However, regardless of whether you are a brand-new business owner, or making $100 million a year, each layer of this pyramid should be part of your overall strategy.

The beauty of this model is that no two people will have the same go-to-market strategy, because each of these layers will be composed of entirely different ingredients based on the individual. So, instead of creating the same type of content every single one of your competitors is creating, you will be building out your own thought leadership, blazing new trails, and pulling away from the crowd.

In the following pages, I will be explaining the Conviction Marketing Pyramid, and then diving deep into how to leverage this model to build the brand you were meant to create. Many entrepreneurs fail to evolve through the three phases of content that I am going to address, dialing into one but never moving on to the others. As a result, they never elevate their brand to the level they could, and they struggle to really stand out.

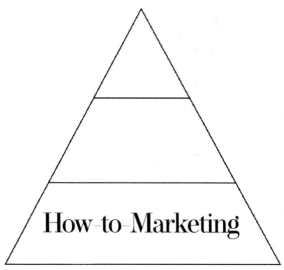

## How-To Marketing

When you start your business, you'll start with simple, how-to content, which is the base of our pyramid. This allows you to build credibility and authority by providing transactional value. Your how-to content shows the market that you are not only knowledgeable, but that you are able to give them information that leads to quick gains. This content can be short form quick tip videos or long form in-depth blog posts or instructional videos. It is designed to teach your followers something that will lead to a small breakthrough, a simple win, or a light bulb moment.

A critical piece of building an online brand with staying power is *trust*. How-to content positions you as a trusted teacher who has valuable information the market needs. It builds credibility, authority, and rapport that often leads to reciprocity with the market. By continually providing high-value, informational content, you create a sense of reciprocity that causes your followers to want to engage and return the favor, often in the form of buying your products or services, sharing your content, or making referrals.

While many entrepreneurs are in a constant cycle of creating how-to content, many fail to elevate their brand because they jump around from topic to topic, without consistently and frequently teaching on the same core topics in order to become truly known for something. One week it's this; the next week it's that; the following week, it's something else. They're trying to address a broad variety of topics, so the market cannot gain a sense of where their real credibility and authority lie. This is why I always stress repetition, consistency, and frequency in the content you are using to build the base of your pyramid. People need to know what you specialize in, what you are the absolute best at, what your zone of genius is, and the subject matter for which you are the go-to person. It should be crystal clear that, when someone needs your specialty, you are top of mind. This is what your how-to marketing should be developing and creating—authority, credibility, and value.

How-to content can take on many forms and can be used on all platforms with the goal of teaching your market something that will help them take a step closer to their goals. It is the foundation of your marketing, because it serves the market in a high-impact way. HOWEVER, the biggest mistake you can make in your marketing is believing that how-to content is enough. It's not.

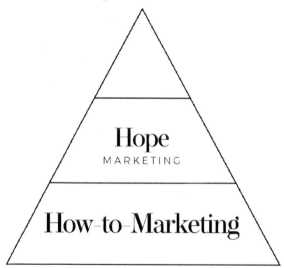

## Offering Hope

When your content strategy stops at informational, you are building on shaky ground. Tactics change, and people will quickly move from one helpful information source to another. If you want to build loyal, raving fans who actually want to buy from you, you need to progress through the next two layers of the pyramid, starting with hope marketing. No matter how much your audience may want to learn the things you know, do the things you do, and get the results you get, "life" is going to happen. This is where hope marketing plays a pivotal role in your market positioning. Hope marketing is instilling inspiration into your market. It's showing up at just the right time for someone who wants to give up and inspiring them to keep going. It's painting a picture of what's possible for someone who is struggling through difficult times. It's reminding people of their potential. It's stepping into the role of trusted mentor and friend vs. simply being a great teacher.

*Your message: Keep believing; you can do this.*

A critical component of effectively infusing hope into your market is empathy. Sharing your own struggles and hardships, both past and present, enables you to establish a deeper connection with your audience. Sharing what you've done to overcome seemingly insurmountable obstacles will encourage your followers to have hope in the midst of their own struggles.

Where how-to is intellectual in nature, hope marketing taps into the emotional side of your ideal clients. You are providing inspiration and fueling their fire. The message is, "We're in this together. I understand and completely empathize with you. We can do this!"

This type of marketing will look different for everyone, since we all come to the table with a unique story. Every market is different in the way it requires infusions of hope. World events and a constantly changing online landscape will introduce new obstacles to tackle and new challenges to overcome.

How-to content alone will not keep your prospects hanging around long-term. There must be an emotional connection for the relationship and loyalty to build, and that is the role of your hope marketing—emotional connection. Ask yourself what your brand must incorporate to create and grow the client-for-life mentality, even before a prospect actually becomes a paying client.

Followers may *come* to you because they want to learn the tips, tricks, tools, and strategies you use and teach. However, they'll *stay* with you because they believe you're someone they like and want to be like. They'll stay because they know that, when they want to give up and quit, you'll be there with the inspiration they need to push through. They'll stay with you because, when they feel the world is against them, you'll post content that motivates them to keep fighting.

They come to you for the how-to, and they stay with you for the emotional connection, the empathetic rapport, and the hope! They won't want to unlink themselves from the progress they've made.

Hope marketing is about stories, inspirational quotes, testimonials, shared client successes, and demonstrations of what is possible. It's about bringing people back to their *why* to spur action, and it's about helping them see the raw potential they have inside of them. This level of your content pyramid is about pulling in massive numbers of people and keeping them engaged and connected.

Let me be honest. There are plenty of people—your competitors—teaching the exact same how-to material that you're teaching. However, very few of them are elevating to the next level of hope marketing in which you really let prospects see behind the curtain and make the necessary emotional connection. Not to mention your story, your client results, and the way you inspire hope can't be copied. They are uniquely yours, so they immediately cause you to stand out.

In my experience, whenever I share a personal tidbit or struggle I've had, I see the highest levels of engagement and get the most feedback. People seem to reach out immediately with that kind of content, even if it's with a simple, "Hey, I hope you're doing okay." There is concrete emotional connection established in those small exchanges. People want to feel like you're human, and when they see glimpses of your humanity, they respond in kind.

Hope marketing brings people back to their why and reconnects them with themselves. How-to marketing places you in the role of teacher. Hope marketing places you in the role of mentor. You've elevated your relationship with them to something that is a lot harder for them to forget. Most entrepreneurs, including your competitors, aren't doing this. They are not going beyond how-to marketing. They are not solidifying their relationships the way you will be once you establish yourself as a mentor.

Hope marketing goes beyond creating just a mentor relationship. Hope marketing puts you on the path to establishing a friendship. Trust increases exponentially. It's much higher than the trust someone may have placed in you at the how-to level. Don't misunderstand—how-to content is essential and critical; it is the base for everything else. But you must also elevate to the next level to begin differentiating yourself from your competition and placing yourself in a category of one.

Hope marketing connects the dots between "I know what to do" and "How do I stay motivated to keep doing it?" When you allow yourself to be vulnerable, your credibility actually explodes. It is the thing that makes prospects see you as someone with whom they want to spend their time and money. You become a person of maturity and wisdom—a person of excellence. Others see you as someone they like and want to be like.

Hope marketing is the second layer in your pyramid. The combination of how-to and hope is magical in elevating your brand, because it creates both value and connection in your relationship with the market.

One important caveat to the discussion about hope marketing is that hope marketing alone, without a direction or call to action, won't get the job done. Without how-to, it will just come across as inauthentic and fluffy. The reason it is the second piece of your marketing is that you must first establish your authority before you start forging deeper connections. Otherwise, you will grow your following full of people who like you, but who don't necessarily see the value in buying something from you, because you won't have any credibility. So, use hope marketing as it was intended, as the second layer of your marketing strategy.

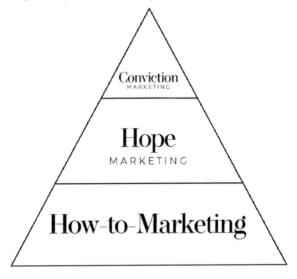

## Reaching the Pinnacle

The third layer is truly the pinnacle of all trailblazing marketing strategies. This is the thing that no one teaches, and very few people ever incorporate. It is exactly why I've written this book. As you move through your business and begin identifying and filling the gap that exists in your industry (I cover the concept of the gap extensively in my previous book, *The Live Launch Method*), and gain clarity about who you are and what is occurring in your marketplace, along with the potential of what *could* be happening, you will begin to realize that, deep down, you have a set of incredibly strong core beliefs.

These beliefs are going to center around what your market deserves and what is possible for your clients and prospects. They will focus on what your clients and prospects could be doing that would create optimal outcomes that no one else in your space, and certainly none of your competitors, has ever offered. You can express these beliefs in a series of statements you have about your industry that you create, write out, codify, teach your team, and go back to again and again. You can post the beliefs publicly like a manifesto on your social media banner or website. You can share these in your videos, on your podcast, and in interviews. These beliefs are going to be what radically sets you apart.

The gap comes back time and time again in terms of exploding your business. Finding the gap in your industry allows you to place yourself into a category of one by becoming the best you can possibly be and filling the gap. Selling to the gap is about going the extra mile.

While the first two levels or rungs of your pyramid are critical to success, they will not elevate you to a category of one. The most crucial part of the pyramid—conviction marketing—is *the place* where you will completely differentiate yourself!

That said, this is also where entrepreneurs can go off the rails and make big mistakes. This is why few businesses ever achieve category-of-one status. Most entrepreneurs have ideas, thoughts, and convictions about what is happening in their respective markets. I see it from business coaches and marketers all the time. They continually blast out their opinions about all the things that are wrong regarding how their competitors are doing business and all the things that are wrong with their marketplace. They shout about the things they dislike and what they see as being a disservice to ideal clients.

> *Having an opinion about what's wrong is entirely different than doing what's right.*

Having an opinion is fine, wonderful even. More power to those who share their opinions publicly. However, having and expressing an opinion about what's *wrong* is unbelievably different than committing to doing what's *right*. Let me repeat: *Having and expressing an opinion about what's wrong is unbelievably different than committing to doing what's right.*

When I look at my company (and if we're not already the fastest-growing business education company in the country, we will be in a matter of months), we've known for years what was wrong in the space and in the market we served; however, I never shared my opinions publicly. I simply experienced it. I went through coaching programs, signed up for courses, and participated in masterminds. I experienced firsthand everything that was wrong, but I didn't yet have the solution.

What I observed happening in current offerings in the market did not actually meet people where they were to get the results they were promised or desired. I saw:

- Big promises of overnight results that were unobtainable for the average person and left entrepreneurs feeling defeated with no path forward

- Thousands of people being cattle-herded into programs with no oversight, direction, or human touch to guide them through

- Out-of-date content that was relevant at one time that the course creators or business owner can't or doesn't keep up with

- Disjointed tactics being taught in a copy-and-paste, plug-and-play format that actually handicaps business owners more than it helps them because it places them in a definitive secondary position

I saw what problems existed, but I didn't know how to perfectly solve them. Additionally, without knowing exactly what the solution looked like, I wasn't fully committed. But I kept having these feelings build and grow inside of me, and it became so much more than building a business for me. I felt called. I began to see that this was my mission, my responsibility, to find the solutions, create the solutions, pioneer a new way of thinking, a new way to deliver on the promises, and therefore making success in entrepreneurship actually viable to the masses, not just a small select few.

I got crystal clear on all that was wrong in the online business education space and challenged myself to imagine what it would look like to make it right. And here are some of the things we knew had to change:

- Entrepreneurs, for the most part, do not have a high-level business background, so they need to be taught timeless business principles, first and foremost, that they will apply to everything they do for the rest of their lives. Then, from there, they can layer in short-term tactics.

- Information is great, but in order to achieve results, people need to IMPLEMENT. For any type of program to create lasting transformation, it needs to go beyond information into a focus on implementation and results.

- People, by nature, are procrastinators, without some form of human touch bringing them back to center and creating "positive pressure" to keep moving forward when the going gets tough.

The list goes on and on, but you get the idea. There was a big old GAP. And, despite the coaching market being one of the most oversaturated spaces online, there was a huge opening in plain sight.

This is why it is so important to lift your head up and observe, be a consumer in your own market, and most importantly, do not get caught up in the story that there is no room or opportunity for you.

There are limitless possibilities for each of us to pause, reflect, and then set out to create solutions that fill a gap in the market. Every industry has multiple gaps, hiding in plain sight, that could be your catalyst to industry leadership.

Taking these observations, I began to imagine what a dream scenario would have been for me as a client when I was joining these programs, courses, and masterminds, and I set out to create it!

We flipped the Unstoppable Entrepreneur program inside out and upside down. Effectively, we took all the things that were wrong with the industry and packaged it into what we believe is right, and we've been doing it, delivering on that promise, ever since.

Here are what the results looked like for our clients when we flipped our concerns into convictions and built the program around it!

1. In just over a year, Jack and Michelle Bosch took their business from 7- to 8-figures.

2. Dr. Avis Jones-DeWeever pivoted from selling on stage to selling online due to the pandemic, and went from 6- to 7- to multiple-7-figures in just over a year.

3. Iva Paleckova, a single mom running her business with a newborn, went from living on government assistance to making over 1 million dollars in one year.

4. Heather Alice Shea added multiple 6-figures to her bottom line in just a handful of launches.

5. Steph Weber retired from her full-time job in 4 months because she was able to fully replace her income.

6. Julie Ciardi retired her husband after decades in law enforcement after creating multiple 6-figure leaps in her business.

7. Kimberly Olson took her online presence from low 6 to over 7 figures in less than a year!

8. Melissa Henault made multiple 6-figure leaps in her business within the course of a year, using *The Live Launch Method*.

9. Samantha St. Louis added 6 figures to her bottom line, with 3 kids under 4, while pregnant with her 4th!

10. Dr. Angela Tran was able to close her 7-figure brick and mortar business and pivot fully online within 2 days when shutdowns happened in early 2020, keeping her full team in place while continuing to grow.

The conviction about what I believed was possible, and the courage to pioneer a new path forward that bucked the trend of over-automation and low/no contact mass market solutions, created an explosion in the market. We went global and the brand began to explode.

When I saw how much the market was craving this, and how it literally sent entrepreneurs into a frenzy, because it was so different from everything else out there, that is when I *knew* I had to begin to document the Conviction Marketing Method for you.

You have these feelings inside of you. You see it; you know it could be so much better, so much different. But maybe it seems too big, or not sexy enough, not shiny enough, not trendy enough. DO IT ANYWAY. At the core, we are all human beings. Whatever it is that your entrepreneurial calling is leading you to do, answer the call. Go all in. Don't play it safe and keep playing the same game your market has been playing for years—be the ONE to introduce a new conversation, an alternate reality.

Then use the stories of success and the beliefs you have in your go-to-market strategy over and over again.

## Fill the GAP Again and Again

You'll hear me teach often about filling the gap and simplifying to multiply. It's what our coaching programs are based on, and it's in every piece of my marketing strategy.

Now is the time for you to take action. I want you to start writing down all of your own opinions about what's wrong in your industry, where the gaps are. Start with what you believe your prospects deserve. Think through the shiny, well-marketed things that are keeping them stuck, and challenge yourself to go at least 10 steps beyond where you think you're capable of going to make everything that is wrong right. Commit to filling a gap. It's not going to be pretty or perfect, and that's okay.

I want you to stop reading and take a few minutes right now to itemize 10 things that you know are wrong, or clearly in need of improvement, in your space. Perhaps you know them right off the top of your head. Take whatever time you need to come up with 10:

1. _____

2. _____

3. _____

4. _____

5. _____

6. _____

7. _____

8. _____

9. _____

10. _____

Give yourself the grace needed to keep honing and developing the best solutions. That is what we did in our endeavor to solve the huge lack of accountability, accessibility, and support that I saw existed in our space. We're trying new things every day of the week to make improvements. We didn't start with a blueprint; we figured it out as we went.

Conviction marketing is, as I said, the pinnacle of all pinnacles. You elevate yourself above the foundation of how-to marketing and then grow beyond your hope marketing content. You begin as the teacher with how-to marketing, and you become the mentor and friend through your hope marketing messages. Conviction marketing catapults you into the status of visionary!

There are plenty of entrepreneurs who have an opinion of what's wrong, but almost no one is willing to implement and execute what it takes to make it right. Be that person.

When you do so—identifying what is wrong and committing to making it right and marketing to that effort with both *problem and solution*—you become the visionary. I want you to literally breathe into existence the future, what's possible, and where your company will fill that GAP to help people achieve their desired end state.

You are creating and setting a new standard of excellence, not only for yourself but for your competitors as well. This is what sets you apart. You are setting a new, higher bar for the future and quite literally reinventing your space. Of course the result is that you become a category of one— peerless!

## Create the Future

Quite frankly, most business owners are not willing to do the work or spend the money needed to solve the problems in their marketplaces. They're not focused enough on the ultimate long game to be willing to invest now to achieve the outcomes they really want later. Are *you*?

If you are willing to go the distance and invest in a new technique up front, this could pay you back in explosive revenue and growth beyond your wildest dreams. **I want to challenge you to elevate yourself from teacher to friend/mentor to visionary leader.**

Take the first step to go the extra mile, both presenting the problem and the solution that no one in your space or industry has done. A visionary sees something that is not yet reality. Visionaries create the future and lead people to it. Define it according to your terms, and this will become branded language people can share on social media.

> *Visionaries CREATE the future and lead people to it.*

Open up your heart, your soul, and your purpose. When you are starting your business, and operating as a small fish in a big pond, it is easy to let what you see as being *wrong* in your market disappoint and frustrate you. You'll see that you are doing things differently—doing things the way your prospects need—but they are still stuck buying according to the old paradigm. Despite that, you have to keep doing what you're doing. You have to allow it to play out. You have to stick to your convictions. Don't change your message. Let your convictions guide you as you live, lead, teach, and serve.

Success won't happen overnight, and success never happens without effort. Keep going with your how-to marketing to gain attention. Keep your prospects hooked with your hope marketing. Then share your powerful and deeply-held convictions in alignment with your commitment to change the world. Take these steps and you will be unmatched in your space.

There is no mystery as to why most businesses will never reach the top and move into this category-of-one status. It's not magic, and there is no fairy dust involved. Neither is it wishful thinking or even talent. There is simply a methodical decision-making process that goes into all of this. If you look at our programming and what we're teaching there and then compare it to what our competitors are doing, you'll see they're attempting to do what we do using only a shell staff—a business owner and a handful of contracted coaches. There's no strategic business advisory, or high level consulting. The focus is solely on tactic vs. the strategic planning and thinking processes required for growth.

| Most Online Business Coaching | Our Consulting |
|---|---|
| FOCUS ON FLEETING TACTICS | TIMELESS BILLION DOLLAR BUSINESS PRINCIPLES APPLIED TO THE ONLINE LANDSCAPE |
| NICHE SPECIFIC | |
| VIRALITY | HIGH LEVEL |
| HOT TAKE OF THE MINUTE | FORWARD THINKING STRATEGY |
| AUTOMATION WITH NO HUMAN SUPPORT | HUMAN CENTRIC SUPPORT |
| | SCALABLE AND SUSTAINABLE PRACTICES |

In the short term, I could run the program with me and a staff of three, collect the revenue, and call it a day. However, I choose to focus on my visionary north star—my purpose, passion, and desire to become the category of one—and reinvest into the client RESULTS division of the company. This ultimately translates into clients winning and creating lasting relationships, referrals, and even greater growth all around.

Every day, I choose the long-term over the short-term. Short-term sacrifice to gain long-term results. That is category-of-one decision making. That is visionary leadership.

We want to be the best in the world at what we do. PERIOD. It is not about a race to the finish line or a grab for someone's credit card. Every day we return to our north star and ask ourselves, "How can we simplify the path to financial freedom for entrepreneurs? How can we make a substantial and lasting difference in the world of entrepreneurship, helping people to achieve levels of success they otherwise would have never reached?" This is what drives me day in and day out.

At every turn, I reiterate to my growing team of 50 full-time employees that we are all here on a mission. Our mission is to be the best and most recognized business education and leadership development company in the world. This mission was largely born from the convictions that I've developed over time.

Every day we are moving aggressively and with certainty, confidence, and conviction in that direction because of three things:

1. We know with absolute certainty where we are going and why; we have a clear target.

2. We are committed to filling the gap and living in a space of never-ending improvement.

3. We have placed ourselves in a category of one utilizing the exact formula and steps I am laying out for you in this book.

## Now it's your turn:

1. Where are you going and why? What is your north star? What is the change you are called to create in your industry or space?

_____

_____

_____

_____

2. What is the gap you will fill? And, for my own students, please remember this is a process you do over and over again—reinvention and renewal of your commitment to create an alternate and better path forward.

_____

_____

---

---

3. Define what it will take to place yourself in a category of one AND what are you willing to do to achieve this.

---

---

---

---

## Establishing Your Convictions

- Your marketing content is a pyramid with three levels: how-to, hope, and conviction messaging.

- Make your base strong with how-to content that builds your credibility and authority. It contains lessons, transactional skills, tips, and strategies. It establishes you as a teacher.

- Consistency and frequency are critical components of any well-established brand.

- Hope marketing embraces empathy and is where you inspire your audience to keep going when things get tough. It establishes you as a mentor and friend.

- People will connect with your how-to marketing, and they'll stick with you because of your hope marketing.

- When you elevate beyond your how-to base, the trust and rapport you build explode.

- Conviction marketing is the pinnacle of pinnacles. It establishes you as a visionary leader and catapults you to category-of-one status.

- Having and expressing an opinion about what's wrong is unbelievably different than committing to doing what's right. Do what's right.

- When you become a visionary leader, you become peerless and are positioned to actually create the future.

# Chapter Three:

# Identifying Your Differentiating Beliefs

*Having faith, beliefs, and convictions is a great thing, but your life is measured by the actions you take based upon them.*

**- Nick Vujicic**

A s we entered 2020, I truly believed that the online marketing world was prime for disruption and that it was time to knock things "back down to a reasonable level." There was an overabundance of "copy and paste" marketing along with what I'll call a silent pressure for those in the online space to do what everyone else does, teach what everyone else teaches, and be like everyone else is. There is zero authenticity in that.

Almost every successful entrepreneur has deep convictions about why they got into business in the first place, what they believe, and the potential they saw in how things "could be." Yet they still felt the pressure to participate. Maybe this resonates with you. You see the potential of how things could be, you see and want to create what's possible, yet you still feel the pressure of what everyone else is doing.

When entrepreneurs see their competitors having success and getting results, they may think they have to replicate what is already being done—addressing the same topics, offering programming in that space, and reflecting that they also are competent. They fear that, without doing so, they won't achieve their growth goals, won't stand out, and won't be taken seriously. This is 100% false!

The whole idea of conviction marketing, and the gift I want to give you in the pages of this book, is for you to embrace the concept of zigging when everyone else zags. I want you to always keep in mind why you started in the first place. I am certain that, when you started, you could clearly see the potential in yourself and in your market. You had a clear vision of what's possible—how things could improve, how things could be better, and how things could evolve—all in a way that could serve the market at a higher level. You believed that you could,—in some way, shape, or form—improve the delivery mechanism, model, or results in the market you serve.

As you began marketing and operating in your space, it's possible you got stuck in a groupthink mindset. Suddenly, you're talking about the same things others are talking about, and you start doing the same things everyone else is doing. Your brand starts reflecting the same things other brands reflect. The problem is that this doesn't underscore who you truly are, what you believe, and what you embrace as the reason you were put on this planet. It does not demonstrate how you can serve your market or the impact you can make.

Recognize that, in a world where there is zero barrier to entry—anyone can set up a social media profile, throw up a bio and picture, and they're in business with little to no cost or investment—the field becomes ripe for groupthink and a copy and paste approach. With that, you are in for an uphill battle! You will always be second best at replicating someone else and their convictions. You can only be first in class when you step forward and shine a light on your own convictions and what you believe.

Here's what is important to understand: entrepreneurs who have deep convictions and powerful ideas about what can change, and how they can impact the world, can become frustrated by competitors who are succeeding without adhering to their own convictions. While those people seem to be influential and generating results, I assure you, your market is waiting and ready for something different. But, because too many entrepreneurs think they have to participate in the cookie cutter marketing world in order to profit, there is an endless cycle of everyone copying everyone else. It becomes a hall of mirrors, and the result is that consumers in many instances are not getting what they want and need.

I'm not suggesting that this is happening intentionally. Most entrepreneurs are doing what they've been taught— that success leaves clues. This is actually true, and there is nothing wrong with observing what a successful person is doing and investing in learning their methods and duplicating them in your own way.

However, you must take the next step in your evolution—certainty and conviction in moving forward as an industry leader—and adapt what you learn to carve out your own unique path.

## Define Your Voice

This chapter is about helping you find your voice. You're in the right place if you have a vague sense that something is wrong in your market space, and know you can be the luminary innovator who changes everything, but you need support crafting the steps to get there.

Remember the list you made of everything that is wrong with your industry? This is your opportunity and your compass. In my case, I realized that there were too many business courses launched promising overnight success to people with little to no business acumen, resulting in failure. As a result, students and customers dropped off, became confused, asked for refunds, and didn't get the transformation they sought.

When you think about why you were put on the planet, who you're here to serve, and the difference you can make, you'll see that "go along to get along" thinking does not serve you in achieving this.

In order to evolve into the next level of thought and industry leadership—becoming peerless and catapulting yourself into a category of one—you need to be a disrupter, an innovator, and a person of value. But most importantly, you must be a person of *conviction*!

In our society, there has been a loss of leading with conviction because having an opinion is often not celebrated or even recognized. Granted, there may be certain topics on which it doesn't make sense for you to voice your opinion. However, you absolutely need to define your voice in the underlying beliefs you hold as it relates to your business, the

> *You will either disrupt your industry or be disrupted. There is no in between.*

ones that represent the whole reason you got into business, and the hills you are willing to die on.

What are those convictions? Rather than focusing on your dissatisfaction with the way your *competitors* are marketing and doing business, consider the ways in which *you* can step into becoming the change. As an entrepreneur, you are a solution provider. What are the solutions you can bring to your industry that are unique to you and your expertise?

And yes, I actually want you to write your answer, so it becomes more clearly defined for you and your market.

_____

_____

_____

_____

_____

_____

_____

_____

I have been teaching for years about filling the gap. Conviction marketing is very much about you finding the gap in your space (and there is at least one gap in every industry!), building your program around that gap, and committing to being the change that will fill the gap. You must determine how you can articulate these beliefs in a compelling way that allows your market to respond with, "Finally! Someone is stepping forward to provide what's been missing."

The danger with "copy and paste" marketing is that consumers continue to purchase subpar products and solutions from individuals who don't really fulfill the highest level of service. When you find yourself stuck here, it is because you have not fully embraced living your own convictions. When you live your conviction, the market will quickly follow. But you have to go first. In much the same way that you started your business, invest in yourself first, and the market will follow. The market is ready for, and wants, conviction and authenticity.

To become the change, and see the market recognize and follow that change, allowing you to step forward as a leader in your industry, you must first step forward with a new and different message, and

> *Zig when everyone else zags. This will always set you apart. Always.*

a commitment to delivering on the outcome. In my case, I actually started talking about and teaching the concept of "social selling" about three years before it was a common phrase. Social selling is the difference between waiting for the market to come to you and you going out and grabbing it. Conviction marketing is very similar. It is you recognizing that you need to start a brand new conversation with your market about what can be, about potential, and about your vision and willingness to commit.

Right now, stop and determine what your primary conviction is. What is the one thing to which you are willing to commit your life and for which you'd burn at the stake?

I am dedicating my life to:

_____

_____

_____

_____

_____

_____

_____

_____

_____

For me, *I am committing my life to simplifying the path to financial freedom through entrepreneurship* because I believe it is harder and more complex than it needs to be. I believe that too many people fail who could certainly succeed. I believe there is a better way.

This is exactly why we flipped the business model two years ago toward implementation and away from simply providing information. As the market continued to move more toward automation and digitizing the consumer experience, business owners continued to struggle and fail with too many dreams headed for the graveyard. I realized that my convictions were exactly what would compel and propel me into a category of one. My convictions about the overreach of automation and the dehumanization that accompanied digitization—exactly why entrepreneurs were failing in the coaching space—have led to my success and elevated me to a thought leader in the industry.

When you think about illuminating your own convictions and starting the important conversation your market needs that no one else is having, are you leaning toward playing it safe and relying on already proven concepts, or are you breaking the mold? Think about the entertainment industry. It's become very formulaic at the expense of creativity and new ideas. New movies don't feel new at all. They all seem to be a remake of a story that's already been told. That industry has wimped out. They're only producing things that already have market validation versus telling a brand new story.

> *It's time to write your own story and stop regurgitating the same old story we've been hearing for years.*

If you are feeling bored, or in a rut of repetition in your own business, you are not alone. One of the things that really burns out entrepreneurs and erodes their sense of purpose is feeling like they're being put into a box. They feel like they have to cover this topic, teach this thing, deliver in a certain way, and follow a particular model. It's exhausting. It's time for you to break out! It's time to follow whatever it is that sets your heart and soul on fire.

Today, I want you to get really excited about something new and about breaking the mold. Embrace what gives you a sense of purpose. I want you to take what is burning inside of you, bring it forth, and allow it to illuminate your market. Shine your light into the world because the world needs it now more than ever. The world needs you—and your market needs you—*right now*.

## Go Higher

The innovations that have occurred in every industry have brought us to the point we're at today, but there is always a next level. In creating that, ask yourself: "Why not me? Why can't I be the person to begin a new conversation that pushes my industry further? Why can't I lead the market in a way that prospects and customers don't even know is possible?"

When we brought the concept of accountability coaching to the market, there was no blueprint. When we ripped apart and destroyed every concept that was being taught in the launch space with *The Live Launch Method*, we didn't know if it was going to work. We simply knew what *didn't* feel good and what *wasn't* working for us, so we had to try things differently. We had to create a breakthrough launch technique that did not require hundreds of thousands of dollars in clunky tech funnels, scattershot Facebook ad formulas, hit-or-miss webinars, and inflated tripwires that leave you with a "successful launch" that has a minuscule profit margin, or worse, doesn't work. We had to become the change.

Embrace that. It's okay to admit that the conversation currently taking place in your market no longer resonates with you. In fact, maybe you're having the same conversation and are no longer excited about it. Maybe you're teaching on topics about which you no longer have passion. Very likely, there's an internal calling for you to bring forth a new set of ideas, but you're holding back because those ideas stray from the current market conversation and supposed successful blueprint. Maybe even stray from what has made you money.

Studies indicate that the most prosperous industries right now include health and wellness, relationships, business, wealth, personal growth, and more. That said, I want you to use your own common sense. I strongly encourage you to be *you*. I want you to listen to your inner calling and illuminate those ideas inside of you that your market has never heard. Maybe you don't think they're powerful enough, important enough, or worth enough. I get it. I fought the same thing for years. Honestly, what I teach now are things I never would have taught when I started. I would not have started that conversation or focused on those topics. I lacked market validation and didn't know if they'd "play."

You have a message that matters. I want you to clearly understand that! Plus, you have a powerful way to bring your message to the world using *The Live Launch Method*. It allows you to have a much-needed two-way conversation with your market in a way you can be authentically *you* while propelling yourself to another level. Every time I deliver a live launch, there is something different about me and my message. While I'm teaching the same concept, I am ultimately a different person because I've grown and evolved. This is truly the power of the live launch—it allows you to grow and unleash what's inside of you without worrying about technology, the email sequence you created, pre-recorded videos, etc.

Instead, *The Live Launch Method* brings you to your moment to have the freedom to be present with your audience and to start leading your market rather than following it. And let's go a level deeper with it. Your live launch is about bringing your own conviction to the forefront. Think of it as a trampoline. Every time you bounce, new ideas spring forth, and every time you leap, you gain greater and greater height. The magic of *The Live Launch Method* is how it enables you to grow and evolve every single time.

Now, you may think you are already showing up to your audience, prospects, and customers with conviction, but I guarantee you, you can go at least one layer deeper—and then another layer after that and then another. There is a message one layer deeper—words that have never come out of your mouth—that I want you to uncover and deliver. *That* is your true conviction.

Speak what you've never spoken before, and share what you've never shared before. When you do, you will powerfully step into a conversation with your market that no one else is having. The whole reason you got into business is because you saw a problem that no one else was solving. Now it's time to commit yourself, your business, and your life to solving it.

The question I get repeatedly is: "How do I stand out?" Honestly, the answer is reasonably simple. You stand out and set yourself apart by having a sense of conviction and real purpose in your business. More importantly, that conviction must supersede the surface-level conversations happening in your industry.

Let me forewarn you: For some of your prospects, your differentiating beliefs and convictions will be over their heads. They will not get it; they will not be on board with you. Is that a problem? No. That is completely okay! You are here to make a difference, and you will not be able to do that for all people. You cannot be everything to everyone, nor do you want to attempt to do so. Stick to your convictions and beliefs, and serve those who understand you at the highest level. There are over seven billion people on the planet. I assure you, there are people who are waiting for *you*, and there are enough of them to fill your programs. People who can't wait to link arms with you because you are exactly what has been missing for them.

## It Starts with You

What rule are you currently living by that it is time to break?

_____

_____

_____

Having conviction is all about breaking the rules, and it's time for you to start doing it. Shatter the ceilings and crush the obstacles you face in your own space, industry, family, or community. The "approved way" is no longer the best way. It's on you to create the best way. It starts with you unleashing your own potential.

Put a stake in the ground, and claim the space as your own.

That became very apparent recently to one of my clients, Dr. Ranelli Williams, CPA. While the business she started with her husband was successful, it started to plateau and was not scaling. She continued to lead with personal finance due to her own backstory. However, that wasn't really the place for her. It lacked authenticity. Ranelli explains, "My expertise is being a CPA. Once I made the pivot to change my program and my group to align with my convictions, it has made such a difference."

The more we lean into who we really are, the easier everything becomes. It was very clear to Ranelli that, when she identified where her focus should be, business boomed.

Where is your focus right now? Where *should* it be? These are critical questions for you to answer to enable you to become the change and lead your market. These are the questions for you to answer to truly define and refine your convictions.

## Establishing Your Convictions

- You can only be the best, and in a category of one, when you stand up for your own convictions rather than imitating someone else.

- There is an endless cycle of everyone copying everyone else. Set yourself apart and break that cycle by identifying the gap and then taking action to fill it.

- When you live your conviction, the market will quickly follow you.

- Conviction marketing, like social selling, is the difference between waiting for the market to come to you and going out and grabbing it.

- Now is the time to break out and follow whatever it is that sets your heart and soul on fire.

- With *The Live Launch Method*, you have the freedom to be present with your audience and lead, rather than follow, your industry. When you combine the Live Launch with Conviction Marketing, you will be unstoppable!

- It truly does start with you. Break the rules. Define the game you want to play, and get on the field. Let's go!

# Chapter Four:

# Creating Messaging that Matters

*"People don't buy what you do; they buy what you stand for."*

**-Simon Sinek**

L et's be honest: your market is not looking for you to put lipstick on a pig. Sounds harsh, but here is what I mean—most buyers are habitual investors in a space, product, or industry. They have seen the dog-and-pony show, and you presenting another variation of "more of the same" isn't going to cut it for a discerning buyer online.

You may not describe your approach as selling to a discerning buyer online, but here is why you should. Consumers are getting smarter and more experienced at sniffing out the BS being sold to them every minute of every day. You can try to shortcut and make a quick buck, but I promise you, there will be no fulfillment, sustainability, or lasting success in that. Not if you plan to be able to succeed online for any period of time and want to attract ideal dream clients. They are habitual buyers that know what they are doing and are willing to pay a premium to get the best solution, not the cheapest one.

They want a complete and total alternate reality—a new and different experience from your industry. They want real RESULTS, and they want to know that your approach uniquely qualifies you to be the solution that is required. They want to see and feel that the way you approach solving their problem, one they have been struggling with for years, is going to be the final and lasting solution once and for all!

When you think about creating messaging that matters, there are a few things to consider, and about which you should have crystal clarity, if you want to catapult your business.

1. How can your unique methodology make a real and lasting difference for your market? You need to paint a compelling, enticing, and all-around irresistible future picture in their minds of what this can and will be in this alternate reality you will create.

2. How can you structure and name your methodology in a way that clearly conveys the power and impact of this work?

3. How can you frame your message and offer in a way that feels tangible and real vs. an idea or tactic that falls into the category of white noise?

Since you are reading this book, I know you already care deeply about the growth and profitability of your business and, more importantly, the difference you can make and the impact of the lasting legacy you will create.

You know your market deserves better and that your competitors have fallen short. You see the gap that exists between what they've been promised and the results they've received, and you know exactly how to fill that gap. So let's get clear about how you can paint a picture of the alternate reality you're creating, including all of the details, feelings, expressions, colors, and textures. What is this new experience going to really look and feel like to your prospects and customers?

One of the best compliments we've ever received is: "You'll have no way to categorize in your mind the experience of the Unstoppable Entrepreneur program because there simply isn't anything like it." That underscores the intention and design of the program. And we were able to do that by being a consumer in our own space.

When you are a consumer in your own space, you can make thoughtful and strategic decisions based on your own actual experiences, so you'll know how your prospects are going to experience your program, product, or service. When you understand their pain, you can learn and begin to understand how to become their true solution. Good enough is not good enough, and good enough will never elevate you to category-of-one status.

Focus on gaining complete clarity about what the final state or outcome is—or looks like—before you begin promoting your message. You must also have a clear picture of how the final state or outcome is going to be very different from anything else your competitors are offering and from anything else your prospects have experienced. Paint this clear picture. We're not looking for a dressed up or repurposed existing message, and neither is your market. In other words, no lipstick on a pig, please.

This isn't about being better than your competition. It is about being *different* and placing yourself in your own lane—that special category of one. You've already read that—and probably heard me say it—many times. I do so because it is so important. I want you to start thinking of yourself as unmatched in your industry, making decisions based on that, and acting in alignment with that mindset.

Before you do any messaging, you have to first commit to creating a far superior experience and outcome for your prospects and customers. Then determine how you are going to create that, making educated and informed decisions. You will be able to make those types of decisions based on being a consumer in your own space, understanding what your prospects feel and experience, and most importantly, by being in tune with your own market.

For us, we are obsessive about doing customer reviews, quarterly surveys, and multiple levels of management reaching out to customers every single day to get feedback, inspiration, and ideas for improvements and areas of focus. It is a never-ending commitment. When you do something similar, you will never have to worry about the competition, because you simply care more. Caring more is my 7-figure influencer model and is a unique paradigm shift and formula that I teach inside the Unstoppable Entrepreneur program.

In the world of entrepreneurship, so many times we complicate, overthink, and just make things harder than they need to be. I see entrepreneurs go from A to Z just to get from point A to point B. Making a commitment to caring more and focusing on neverending improvement is a path YOU WILL ALWAYS WIN WITH. It does not hinge on the latest greatest tactic, social media algorithm, or hottest trend. It is a way of being, thinking, and acting that will ensure you always have a competitive edge. Translate this and insert it into everything you do, and it will be like putting on glasses for the very first time. Things will become crystal clear instantly.

## Reality vs. Theory

By caring more and committing to taking the actions that align with that, you can easily create messaging that matters and marketing that stands out, because it comes from a place of understanding, empathy, and the ability to deliver something unique and useful.

It is quite difficult to do business "theoretically." Entrepreneurs want to always make decisions correctly the first time; they want things to play out perfectly; they want things to line up exactly. And everyone wants it right away and on the very first try. That sounds good in theory, but it is impossible. The smaller the box into which you place yourself in terms of taking perfect action, the more difficult you make things for yourself, and the further your messaging will land from where you really want it to be. Instead, I want you to enjoy the huge playground of imperfect action.

*Don't wait for clarity to take action. Action is what brings clarity.*

The more you take imperfect action, the more you are learning and improving. You are gaining in-the-trenches experience with your market and audience. With that knowledge and experience, it will become easier to deliver a superior program, product, or service because you become interconnected, and that leads to a fluid conversation which ultimately becomes your message.

Really go deep, and become obsessed with the concept of the customer journey. Focus on listening, seeking, learning, and understanding. Ask what your prospects' and customers' experiences are. Once you do that, you'll separate yourself from your competitors because they won't actually be your competition any longer. You will be in that desired category of one, competing only against yourself. Your competitors simply become a source of data for you to learn what prospects' biggest frustrations, disappointments, and unsolved pain points are. Your messaging can then speak directly to those.

Take a few moments right now to begin listing what you know to be your customers' pain points:

- _____
- _____
- _____
- _____
- _____
- _____

You can continue to add to the list as you continue to ask questions and learn more about your customers' existing experiences and what it is they really want to achieve that you are able to deliver on. Bake these pain points into your messaging and the solutions that you offer.

## Say It Once; Say It Twice; Say It Again

No matter how long you've been in business—brand new to many years—the most important thing about your messaging is that it must be consistent. The number one mistake that entrepreneurs new to the online space make, that erodes their authority and ability to be taken seriously, is constantly changing their message.

*Without consistency, frequency and clarity, you will never claim REAL authority in the market.*

It is critical to your success to establish a flagship offer, whatever that may be, and go to the market with that one thing. Then consistently teach on the same principles or pillars. If you opt for a "flavor of the week" approach, you are completely undermining the idea of conviction. Repetition is the basis of learning, and teaching your market how to think, by using repetition, is what sets you apart. You must establish yourself and stand on that; you cannot look to your market for the topics on which you should be teaching. You are there to *lead* the market and show the path forward.

Conviction marketing will be relevant well into the future—as long as it is coupled with repetition, consistency, and frequency. You cannot show up once every month and expect to generate results and establish yourself as a thought and industry leader. I fully believe that conviction marketing is the future of online marketing; however, its power is only unleashed when you include consistency, repetition, and frequency. Without those, you cannot claim authority.

You must keep going with the message about your convictions until it sticks. I personally don't look for validation. I don't track analytics. I don't care. My husband jokingly suggests that the part of my brain that needs validation is missing. I'm okay with that. Instead, I am operating from my own deep-seated convictions. It doesn't matter if the market isn't where I am. I am going to keep teaching and repeating until it catches up.

Now, I'm not suggesting that you should ignore common sense. Not at all. You must first be solving an urgent problem. Sell to the urgent need. But you don't have to sell to that need the same way everyone else does. No matter how you share your message, you must absolutely love the topics you cover.

For those of you who are multi-passionate, and this sounds absolutely horrendous, let me give you a perspective shift. I own four companies and a philanthropic foundation. Each is unique; each allows me to live out a piece of my life's purpose; and each is also crystal clear about its unique message to market, the gap it fills, and the difference it makes.

I am not suggesting you can't create and deliver all of the offers that excite you or pursue all the business ideas that bring you joy. What I am instead suggesting is that you have a methodical approach that will allow you to succeed long-term.

For example, with your offers, instead of going to market with five different messages, simultaneously follow a strategic chronological order of go-to-market delivery that flows organically one into the next, into the next.

## Example:

**Step 1:** Go to market with your flagship offering. Scale it up over 12-36 months.

**Step 2:** As the first group is completing the flagship program, that you want to retain and keep as a long-term client, create your ascension offer. What is the new problem they are facing as a result of having success in your program? That now becomes your ascension offer.

**Step 3:** Create your downsell into a lower-level continuity, content-only, maintenance-style membership, or less expensive program that you can easily create high volume in. This now becomes your 3rd offer that allows you to capture low-lying fruit and dollars you would have missed out on otherwise, because they want to work with you but are not ready or able to afford your flagship yet!

**Step 4:** Create your cross sell offers. For me, this started in the other companies I created, but they can be partnerships, affiliate relationships, digital products, or alternate programs once the team and business maturity are in place to support it.

Consistency, clarity, repetition, and frequency of messages DO NOT restrict your ability to be creative or multi-passionate. It allows you to categorize and strategize your message to market in such a way that you can be recognized as an authority and industry leader.

Most people try to go to market with too many offers too soon and their message and marketing become so diluted that it actually loses sales instead of creating them.

Create clarity, scalability, and stability in your messaging and delivery first in a systematic way, then expand, multiply, and duplicate in the other areas you are passionate about.

## Messaging Dos and Don'ts

The first thing to keep in mind in creating messaging that matters is that **it is not about you.** It's about your prospects and customers. It is *always* about them. Too many times entrepreneurs get stuck in imposter syndrome or analysis paralysis trying to get it "right" or "perfect," because they are thinking about how they feel and letting their ego stand in the way of being of the highest service.

Focus first on **being of service and taking imperfect action** that will make a difference for your audience.

Second, find a way to **frame your methodology** or formula in a way your audience can easily understand. Chances are, there is a methodology, a chronological order of the steps you lead people through, or a pathway you use to facilitate progress. Instead of just describing how unique, powerful, or different your message is, really show that it is a well-thought-out framework done in a specific way over and over again to produce a specific outcome.

An easy way to think about framing your methodology is to either draw a simple picture representing how it works OR write out a 3-5-step process that you follow.

Take this space below and actually write out the pillars of your process that you can use to frame and explain your method.

Pillar 1:

Pillar 2:

Pillar 3:

Pillar 4:

Is there a way to physically represent in a drawing or diagram how this process works?

See the example again of the simple triangle below that explains the conviction marketing method. IT IS SO SIMPLE, yet life-changing, for anyone who "gets it."

(insert triangle)

Now, below, I want you to challenge yourself to create a physical representation of your method. This makes it tangible, more valuable, easier to teach with, and easier to sell. It is an asset that clarifies and substantiates what you are teaching in a digital world where it is hard for people to feel as if they are buying something "real."

Third, **name your methodology**, and be specific in articulating what the difference is between what you are showing and teaching them vs. everything else they have learned or experienced up until now. Giving your methodology a name matters because it distinguishes what you are teaching, clarifies the space you are claiming, and creates a memorable lasting impression of you, your business, and your brand.

I find it fascinating that entrepreneurs obsess over their product and program names, yet don't think twice about creating formulas, methods, and processes that are attributed to their business, legacy, and brand.

I have always focused the majority of my attention and energy on teaching. My business has exploded year after year, and we are now the leaders in the business education space. This came as a result of relentless focus on deliberate daily value add to the market. I want to challenge you to think bigger than the next client, bigger than the next launch or new program. Think boldly about the massive lasting legacy you want to create.

The online space trains you to think that, if you don't get instant ROI, you are doing it wrong. Watching and absorbing Instagram stories and social media posts can be toxic to your mental game, because it can cause you to become confused as to why you are not living the laptop lifestyle, jet-setting around the world quite yet. I want you to think critically and research the lives and stories of those who have actually achieved the level of success you desire. Usually, those stories include decades of failure, false starts, and tough learnings. They also often contain years and years of giving more than they received. However, and most importantly, they focused on creating a lasting legacy of impact vs. a quick transaction.

When you get serious about creating the methodology that your messaging is built around, frame it in a way that commands value, and name it in a memorable way, you will STAND OUT. When people play the long game, it is instantly recognizable in their brand, and there is trust created that simply can't be faked.

Serve first; show up for your people; be more concerned about making a deposit in the reciprocity bank than making a withdrawal, and I promise the outcome will exceed your wildest expectations.

When you focus first on being of service, and then work diligently to identify how to communicate your message in a SIMPLE yet powerful way, your audience will lean in and be excited to learn more.

A few don'ts on the other hand:

1. A negative message does nothing to benefit you and your business. Instead, focus on how you will deliver results and a superior outcome. Paint a compelling future vision rather than negatively portraying the past or present. It is okay to compare and contrast and explain why another way doesn't work; just keep it on the up and up. As you scale up into the millions, your competitors will become your most important collaborators, so keep the long term in mind.

2. Don't speak in theoretical or abstract language that people need to decode. You have three seconds to capture and keep their attention.

3. Stop using industry jargon or scholastic terminology and references. This is a huge turnoff for the average person who is counting on you to decode this stuff, not perpetuate their confusion.

A confused mind says NO, so whether your goal is to get someone to become a fan of the brand, an ambassador in the market, or a paying customer, remember your job is to keep it simple and help them understand in no uncertain terms what to do next!

When you remember these simple rules, you are setting yourself up for success in creating messaging that matters and makes a massive impact.

When we created *The Live Launch Method*, we worked tirelessly to build global name recognition. We were very thoughtful about each of the messaging dos and don'ts I just covered. We knew our messaging had to include the idea that all of the experience and knowledge gained from failure—and all of the hard work to get things back on track—had to be a part of creating the change. We hear repeatedly from customers who go through *The Live Launch Method*: "This is the first time I've had fun in my business. This is the first time I've gotten paid what I'm worth. This is the first time I have clarity about achieving my ultimate revenue goal."

We have so many clients who've been able to resign from their full-time jobs, pay off their mortgages, enable their spouses to retire, completely get out of debt—and that list goes on and on. People's lives have changed dramatically because I was unwilling to accept that the antiquated and overly-complex launch models that were being taught were the right approach. I knew they didn't work for most entrepreneurs. They didn't work for me. My conviction was so deep and so strong that there had to be a better way. I knew I could not only paint this picture of an alternate reality; I could create it.

The success my clients had with their live launches only deepened my conviction about it and ultimately led me to write this book. When you understand the *Live Launch Method* and the Conviction Marketing Method and bring them together, you create absolute freedom to be yourself, serve in a way that feels right to you, and make millions in the process.

## Establishing Your Convictions

- Effective messaging is about creating simple, easy-to-understand breakthroughs.

- Before you write one word in your messaging, first commit to creating and providing a superior experience and outcome.

- Attempting perfection makes things difficult. Instead, enjoy the huge playground of imperfect action.

- Messaging must be consistent and repeated frequently.

- Effective messaging is never negative. Don't complain about what is and put down the competition.

- Your message must clearly underscore your conviction.

# Chapter Five:

# Turn Your Convictions into a Tribe Mentality

*"Leaders lead when they take positions, when they connect with their tribes, and when they help the tribe connect to itself."*

**- Seth Godin**

How do you take conviction marketing and create a bona fide movement at scale? This is all about the culture and identity you infuse into your company through your team. In the last chapter, we discussed the development of your customer-facing messaging strategy. In this chapter, we will go deeper into the principles behind the message. We will discuss how to distribute the messaging plan and build a company culture that will rally your team to support your vision and ignite an actual industry movement of disruption.

In any company, large or small, its culture leadership will make or break the organization. As I covered in the last chapter, consistency and repetition of serving in a massive, committed way will establish a culture that allows your clients to thrive. Being centered and anchored in your messaging is fundamental to creating your reputation and communicating your convictions. In order to be a global force, you have to market at that level, and you need to build your community at that level. Your tribe is your stickiness factor that builds your brand and ultimately your legacy.

Legacy is the impact you make that carries on long after you're gone. This is why conviction marketing is the business-building method that has the highest level of integrity. When you operate with the end in mind—the point at which you'd look back at your life and the lives you changed and the difference you made—everything should be in alignment.

When you start with the end in mind, and are firm in your convictions, there will be complete continuity in your business-building strategies. Your sales, marketing, and delivery will be 100 percent in integrity and 100 percent in alignment from the start. This feeds directly into building your category-of-one reputation that will precede you in the marketplace.

When I refer to "tribe mentality," what I want you to think about is community. But not just any community, a fiercely loyal community, one that would go to the ends of the earth for you.

You've probably heard the concept of "a thousand true fans" that began in the music industry. The die-hard fans who not only attend the concert, but buy the VIP seats, the merchandise, and every record. I think about a thousand true fans in the business industry and how that concept translates to those with service-based offers. Coaches should have packages that sell at $10,000 to $100,000 (and if you don't have that yet, I invite you to join one of our business education programs at www.kellyroachcoaching.com and you will be making those sales like hotcakes). When you have a package that's $10,000, you only need to sell 100 of those packages to add an additional *million dollars* to your revenue. Let that sink in. You only have to make 100 sales at that level to have an additional million!

When thinking about your business goals, the stickiness factor becomes very important in achieving those 100 sales. When someone finds you, they're going to stick with you, listen to all of your content, buy everything you offer, be a part of everything you do. They are your true fan. Lifetime value of a customer matters. Instead of a customer being worth $10,000, they may be worth five or six times that amount over the course of their relationship with you. And it goes further than that—they tell friends, family, and colleagues about you.

In a world that is changing moment to moment, and is obsessed with instant gratification, you need an actual strategy to create and sustain long-term relationships.

If you want a community that sticks around long-term and invests in your products, programs, and services over and over again, you need a strategy. This begins with creating a compelling experience in which they feel poured into and supported, and have a true sense of belonging. When you think about your community, think about how they are receiving hope, how-to, and conviction marketing deposits from you each week.

## Rage

There are some critical components of building a community of wildly loyal fans. And having something that they feel unified against is a piece of this.

In every drama, story, or movie, there is a villain, and there is a hero. The story unfolds as these two battle it out, and good overcomes evil (usually). In order to build community, you want to ensure there is a shared villain. Your villain should be a "what," not a "who." It's the systems that don't work, the broken industry norms, the internal feelings of doubt keeping your people from success, not a particular person.

When your followers look at everything they've been through, experienced, and felt, they have to have a reason for it. Why **aren't** they where they want to be? Why have things been so hard? When there is a common villain, it gives meaning to past failures and keeps hope alive. If they believe it just won't work for them no matter what they do, they are never going to invest in another solution, and will ultimately stay stuck. A shared villain allows people to move from "I don't know if this will ever work for me," to "I know why this didn't work and am ready to try again."

For example, when we brought the *Live Launch Method* to market, the villain was the traditional launch methodology in the online marketing world. It was very complex, tech-heavy funnels

> *Something to rage against can ultimately lead to hope for the future.*

with thousands of dollars and tons of time spent on overly-produced videos, and hundreds of emails. It was clunky, difficult to understand, and incredibly expensive on the front end. It took too much time, and the payoff was non-existent. You needed to sell hundreds of people into your course just to break even. It was not designed for everyday entrepreneurs without massive audiences.

I created the *Live Launch Method* to simplify the entire process—cutting out the junk and eliminating the rage-worthy barriers. Everything I gave them to rage against is exactly why they've struggled in the past. I taught them how the old model kept them from experiencing success. It was a common enemy to blame for a very real struggle.

My tribe is now raging against the deep complexity and heavy burden of all the tech they were previously under, along with the lack of authenticity the old launch model created. I am not disparaging anyone or any other company, putting anyone down or naming names. I am simply pointing people to a broken system that truly keeps them stuck, and showing them it's not their fault if it wasn't working out how they had hoped. I have pointed them in the direction of the real villain, and we are fighting against it together.

What can you get people to rage against in your own industry or space? A clear, honest, and definitive reason that creates pain for them:

_____

_____

_____

_____

_____

_____

_____

Giving your tribe clarity about what it is they should rage against is critical to providing the clarity they need to move forward.

# Rally

Of course, now you have to give them something to rally around, something to be hopeful and excited about! You need to provide something they can look forward to and believe in. People will make investments only when they feel emotionally connected, energized, and positive about the future. Help them see the potential for their future and believe that, by linking arms with you and your team, they will achieve ultimate success.

The alternate reality you've created, and are presenting to them as a possibility, is the rallying point. Again, using the *Live Launch Method* as the perfect example, I give people the opportunity to show up and be authentic as a true servant leader. They can be completely in integrity, have fun and feel good, and make a "crap ton" of money doing it. It is an ideal rallying point, because what entrepreneur doesn't want that? Conversely, too many are stuck compromising their quality of life in their attempts to be financially successful, or they compromise revenue potential to have the quality of life they want. You can have both, and my tribe rallies around that idea.

When you think about creating something for your community to rally around, simply ask yourself what the ultimate end goal is that they want to accomplish.

Make sure you clearly and repetitively show them specific examples of how you are helping other people just like them to achieve these outcomes. This is not just when you are trying to sell something. In your messaging, marketing, and overall conversation with your market, be sure that stories and case studies are a centerpiece of the conversation.

Examples of how you can do this ongoing in your community:

- Client spotlights where you do posts, stories, and videos sharing your clients' wins, breakthroughs, and results

- Bringing clients on as guest experts in your community, sharing what they learned, the results they are getting, and how others can too by working with you

- Interviewing your clients on your podcast, on your social media channels, and during the sales period of your launches

What can you give your tribe to rally around? What sets you apart that is the ideal rallying point for your customers?

_____

_____

_____

_____

_____

_____

I teach incessantly about human connection as our superpower. Simplicity is the key to duplicating, multiplying, and scaling. Clarity is what allows you to drive specific outcomes in a predictable, scalable way. You need to first get clear around what you are getting your audience to rally around—and rage against—and then and only then can you create a definitive plan to create this outcome.

Help them get crystal clear on why they weren't getting results before (the rage) and what they need to do now (the rally) in order to create their ideal outcome.

## Tribe Language

You want to really consider words, phrases, analogies, stories, belief systems, and mindsets that are repeated over and over, so they become the cultural foundation of your tribe. They become part of everyone's collective lingo and language as well as becoming part of their thought processes and actual experiences. It becomes the framework through which they see the world. The result is life-changing for them and for you.

Think of ways to get your followers thinking, "This is my club, my tribe, my vibe. These are the people I want to spend time with and who represent my values."

In my case, we use language like "simplify to multiply," "UE revolution," "Live Launch revolution." It specifically gets people energized to *revolt* against complexity and the barriers that prevent business owners from succeeding.

"Cash comfortable" is another phrase we use in my tribe. The *Live Launch Method* is a low-cost, no-barrier-to-entry launch strategy that is incredibly simple to execute and delivers real results. We teach that serving, being in integrity, and coming from a place of kindness and support leads to success. When you establish that and deliver on your promise, you can get results you've never imagined. You quickly become "cash comfortable."

"Unstoppable" is another keyword in our tribe. For my tribe, they know it means that, despite any obstacle, any setback, or anything that stands in their way, they are so committed and anchored and believe so deeply in the value of their life and the opportunity to accomplish their goals and dreams, that nothing will prevent them from fulfilling their highest potential and living in alignment with their purpose. That's a lot packed into one word, yet our entire tribe and brand are built on this word. The result is that we attract very positive, type-A people. We attract the dreamers and the doers, so the culture continues to strengthen, and success explodes.

"Business athlete" is another word we use in our community. We are known as the millionaire makers and attract those who look at their business as a legacy. This means that our people are business owners who are serious about their craft and willing to train for their business like an athlete trains for their sport. We want to work with elite business owners that go the extra mile and are willing to put in the work to achieve 1% results. We are clear about who we are for and who we are not for. We are not a community for dabblers or hobbyists; we are for impact players taking their business to the top. No matter where they are today, it's about their commitment to what they are creating for tomorrow.

Think about the culture and the people you want to attract to your program, product, or service—and the language that underscores it. What words or phrases capture its essence?

- _____
- _____
- _____
- _____
- _____
- _____

Do these words and phrases generate the stickiness factor that will make your prospects and customers develop an unbreakable loyalty? Do they resonate with your own authenticity? Do they make your tribe say, "I belong here and I never want to leave?"

Creating community isn't simply about getting people to attach to you. You want them to attach to one another, supporting and helping each other. They believe in each other and feel connected to one another.

## Seal It

Human connection is your superpower, and it's the same thing that seals your tribe mentality. When you dig deep into the psyche, you build a mentality that sticks with people. Entrepreneurs want to surround themselves with "yes I can" people and a community of others doing what they want to do and achieving what they want to achieve. If not, they will want to give up when the going gets tough. A tight-knit community keeps them in the game, working toward their goals, and honestly, that is exactly what you want to happen.

The absolute conviction about who you are as a company, who you are as a brand, and what you stand for, is the foundation of all your success. Couple that conviction with repetition, the imperfect action you take, the never-ending improvements, and then follow through on delivering beyond-belief results, and you will find yourself more than "cash comfortable."

## Establishing Your Convictions

- When you consider your legacy from the start and are firm in your convictions, continuity in your strategy and messaging becomes organic.

- In building community, your tribe needs something to rage against and also something to rally around!

- Develop words and phrases that resonate with your tribe that they'll adopt as their own and ultimately share and perpetuate, helping you build the brand.

- Creating a community builds long-term brand value which allows for sustainable business growth no matter where you go and what you do from here.

# Chapter Six:

# The Fortune Is in the Follow-Through

*"It was character that got us out of bed, commitment that moved us into action, and discipline that enabled us to follow through."*

**-Zig Ziglar**

Conviction marketing is all about being the catalyst to lead your prospects and customers to transformational change. It's about making your life's work serving and filling the gap in your industry. It is an unwavering and never ending commitment to helping your customers achieve superior results.

Conviction is about stretching yourself beyond the over-promise, under-deliver culture we live in and truly committing to going the extra mile in everything you deliver to the market and to your customers.

When you think about conviction, I want you to make a deep connection to following through from the message to market all the way to the never ending improvement in your product, program, and service delivery.

Conviction is a lifetime commitment to being the change you want to see in the world and going to whatever lengths necessary to make your business and brand category-of-one because the work is simply peerless.

As I write this, we just went through over a year of restrictions, lockdowns, and loss due to the 2020-2021 pandemic. Many cultural shifts and norms have changed and, for many, this was a year full of struggle and immense loss personally and professionally.

However, as a positive, just as with any disruption, it has also created an openness to new ideas, transformation, and innovation. The world is currently shifting at a speed that is difficult to comprehend. We have to make a definitive decision to capitalize on the changes vs. getting taken down by the tidal wave.

Now, more than ever, it's important to pick our heads up and really observe and absorb the things that are occurring in industries outside of our own. Why? Cross-industry collaboration, as well as idea exchanges between colleagues and even competitors, are key to innovation. Industries adopt and follow what other industries—and their competitors—are doing, perhaps with a slight or even substantial variation.

This is where conviction comes into play and why it is so important. Your prospects and customers are not looking for a subpar variation of what they've already experienced.

They want something completely new that allows them to move forward as they never have before. As I've said, they are looking for you to paint a picture of a compelling future along with the pathway to achieve it!

Inside of the Unstoppable Entrepreneur program, we have members from all over the world, from hundreds of different industries. We don't "specialize" in a particular niche industry or business type, and we never will. It's how we've designed the program so that members can enjoy and capitalize on the cross-pollination of ideas that occur when various industries come together. Many businesses fail when they refuse to change, innovate, or reinvent themselves in time. They then get disrupted instead of being the disruptor, and that usually doesn't end well.

Take time to observe and absorb different business types and models. What inspiration and innovation can you draw from them that enables you to color outside the lines and bring a sense of reinvention to your own business?

Always be on the lookout for best practices, no matter what the industry, and determine how you can apply them in unique ways. Your competitors are not doing this, so this is another way to elevate yourself into a category of one. It enables you to sell to the gap. I want you to break the rules and color outside the lines. I want you to do something that hasn't been done before.

In the online space, almost all educational and coaching programs, courses, and masterminds focus on one niche and one industry/business type. If you do not currently have a circle of influence, including people that are where you want to be in all different modalities, I would encourage you to look for a community, mastermind, or coaching program that provides this exposure—it is critical to fuel creativity, innovation, and exchange of powerful ideas.

## Providing a Superior Product

There are opinions and there are convictions. Anyone and everyone has an opinion, and those opinions are generally worthless. On the other hand, when you are committed to serving the gap and building a product or service to meet that need, you are providing real value.

It may be slow at first, because you are presenting new and different ideas that your prospects must begin to understand, but ultimately your program will supersede and outperform what else is available. As Elon Musk recently suggested, entrepreneurs need to put down their marketing Powerpoint presentations and instead get to work improving their products. Tesla is obsessed with creating a superior product, and yes, it's taken a while to become the household name that it is now, but they are clearly at the top of their industry. Their success is founded on their ability to fill the gap.

Stop and consider why your competitors have not filled the gap that exists in your industry. There are usually two reasons: it's expensive and it's hard. Admittedly, I don't always have the best news to share as a business strategist, and I know the most valuable advice I provide isn't the easiest or the most fun. You have to decide your level of commitment to re-inventing your industry in order to achieve the highest levels of success. If you're playing the long game, and you want to achieve excellence, you simply have to do the hard work and make the necessary investments. There is always sacrifice up front; however, when managed correctly, that sacrifice creates massive output and the financial gain that goes with it. When you choose to take on what's difficult and expensive, you automatically eliminate your competition.

> *If success was easy, everyone would be successful.*

## Do Something Extraordinary

If you are going to work this hard, you might as well do something extraordinary! The fortune really is in the follow-through. Anyone can slap together a quick product or course that they want to turn into an income stream. In following through, you must evaluate your idea from every angle to maximize the possibilities and deliver the greatest value with excellence.

One of the big concerns with taking on the "gap" in your industry, as I mentioned above, is that it can be expensive, and here is what I mean. In the world of business education and consulting, many times the business owner uses part-time contracted staff who often have other gigs or businesses. It is almost impossible for a contractor to have the depth of knowledge and expertise required to support clients through the actual programming they invested in. Therefore most consumers in the business education space are left with a bad taste in their mouths, because they invest with high hopes and big dreams just to be left high and dry when they have a question and need live support to get it answered. For us, a big piece of filling the gap was building out a full-time internal team to support the needs of our clients. Instead of competing in the market based on price, we strategically positioned ourselves to actually be the more expensive option and compete strictly on value. This allowed us to invest in the full-time staff required to WOW our clients and break industry norms for success rates. Remember, there is a solution to every problem and, when you think outside the box, you can create a win-win for all involved.

When you compete on price and automation, you are entering the race to the bottom. Someone will always go a dollar cheaper. And the prospects who are attracted by that are not the ones you want anyway!

Instead, position yourself in the top tier. Your pricing should be in the top quartile. Remember that becoming extraordinary is expensive. Pricing properly allows you to invest in the resources you need to create a superior product that is worth every penny of your high-ticket price.

The gap is usually created by accessibility, service, delivery, and accountability—think scalable intimacy. And yes, those are hard and expensive to deliver, but ultimately, they get results.

In developing your follow-through, ask this question: *In a perfect world, if I were a consumer of my own product, what would it look like, and what would I need to put in place to generate the superior results I want on every level?*

Dream it. Imagine it. And now, ***write it down***:

_____

_____

_____

_____

_____

_____

_____

What do the components of your product, service, or program look like?

What changes can you make right now to make it truly world-class?

Where do you see competitors cutting corners or missing the mark where you could really make a difference?

As a consumer in your own space, I imagine you can quickly and easily write down what those big, big gaps are and the reasons why you struggle to get the best result. Take a moment to write down the reasons you didn't get the results you wanted in the past, and reverse engineer your own program to address and deliver those results to your current market.

When you are designing a flagship offer to fill the gap and revolutionize your industry—creating a movement that impacts millions—remember that every "overnight success" was likely 10 or 15 years in the making.

In the case of the Unstoppable Entrepreneur program—which I wholeheartedly believe to be the number-one business incubator on the planet—I started with just myself and three clients on a conference line (Zoom wasn't a thing). Now we serve hundreds of members who are making 6-figure leaps in their revenue, faster and faster, over and over. We now consistently create million-dollar businesses and have even started helping our clients achieve the ever-illusive 8-figure mark. This did not happen overnight; it happened over a period of years. We have disrupted ourselves over and over again in order to beat our best and keep improving.

> *Every overnight success is 15 years in the making.*

Patience, along with hard work and continued investment in yourself and your business, is part of the follow-through process to create transformational change, not only for yourself but for each of your prospects and customers, and that is synchronous with being an industry icon and movement maker. This is a critical component of conviction marketing. Get rich quick schemes and conviction marketing will never coexist. The former is the race to the bottom while the latter elevates you to the pinnacle. You can be certain, if you haven't already experienced this yourself, those "instant breakthroughs" always deliver subpar results.

If you dream of being a movement maker and rule breaker in your industry, you are absolutely capable of doing so. You can create the change your market needs. There is nothing standing in your way, but you must be prepared for the journey. I won't even say it's a marathon over a sprint, because it may likely be longer than a marathon. My journey was 15 years. Never stop investing in yourself and your business. When I launched my first 12-month program, this approach was unheard of. Everything else was "total life and business transformation" in 6 weeks or less, which I always found laughable. True life transformation takes time, repetition, and patience, and I knew that to do something truly extraordinary I needed an approach that matched that.

It took me a few years, but the idea took hold and began to scale. I stood my ground and helped hundreds and hundreds of entrepreneurs understand why this was filling the gap and necessary to gain the results they wanted. It is simply incomparable to everything else, and that is exactly what I want you to do in your own space.

Dare to dream so much bigger than what can be accomplished "overnight" and commit to the follow-through that's needed. Commit to hard work and investment. That's what allows you to enable your own clients to achieve the transformation they desire. And that's exactly where your fortune is. Trust yourself and give yourself the patience and grace for the follow-through you need to become peerless. Creating a superior product will be more than worth it.

## Establishing Your Convictions

- Cross-industry collaboration and idea exchanges create big breakthroughs. Look for opportunities to explore new frontiers.

- Creating a world-class product that matches your convictions is the key to rising to the top.

- In following through, evaluate your offer and idea from every angle; never stop improving.

- Always compete on value, not on price.

- Consider your program as a consumer in your own space; consider the reasons results do not happen, and then reverse engineer the process to ensure they do.

# Chapter Seven:

# Revolt Against the Norms

*"Always take a stand for yourself, your values.*
*You're defined by what you stand for."*

## - Oprah Winfrey

Revolting against the norms—and making millions in the process—will catapult you into a trailblazing category of one.

Revolting against the norms is the differentiator between the entrepreneurs who play small—and will stay small—and those who will elevate to become industry icons.

Let's dive into those key distinctions. Stepping out of the norm is a key part of conviction marketing. It is applicable in any business and any space. We all face times when we may feel we're producing "vanilla" content and are less than excited about what we're doing. When you look at your content and assets and think, "Hmmm, this looks and feels like everyone else," it is definitely time to disrupt and reinvent yourself.

So, how do you cut through the noise, rise above the competition, and stand out?

First, you need an avatar—knowing who you are here to serve, and exactly what your purpose is, will be critical to gaining clarity. A targeted focus is a must; however, you'll never hear me teach about "niching down." Why? First, it causes you to get stuck and may end up costing you thousands (or hundreds of thousands) of dollars. And second, it limits your ability to think outside the box and revolt against the norms of your industry.

Please do not confuse what I am saying with encouraging a lack of focus or clarity about who you serve. I am instead pointing out that, for most entrepreneurs, this is a massive setback in the natural progression of your business. We've talked so many times in this book about how you can't build a business in theory. However, niching down before getting in there and doing the work *is* theory. It is 100% okay to start serving a wide range of clients and begin to narrow your focus as you get more and more clear about who you can help, and how you can help them. Prematurely niching down is a quick way to stunt your business growth.

If you wonder why you are not standing out, it's likely because you are subconsciously absorbing the "groupthink" mentality of your industry. You begin to look, think, and talk like everyone in your market. You're falsely led to believe that this is what your audience wants. If everyone else is doing it, it must be right. Wrong. In doing so, you are falling victim to unconscious bias and conforming to your own industry norms.

I have not niched down my own business to serve a specific industry. My goal is to go *against* industry norms, so the last thing I would do or recommend is that you niche down and align within your industry. Looking to different industries presents new ideas, novel models, and different approaches. There is power in diversity!

Revolting against the norms is about stepping away from what everyone else is doing and allowing yourself to look inside to see what you intuitively know you want to do and how you want to serve. For me, when I was really ready to start scaling my company into the millions, I knew I had to completely disconnect from my competition. I stopped watching their social media, got off their email lists, and stopped listening to their podcasts. I wanted to have a clean palate to operate from instinct, intuition, and heart, rather than unknowingly be influenced by what my competitors were doing around me. This helped me explode my creativity and gave me the freedom to make my business unique to me.

If you are finding yourself sometimes bored with what you are creating, it might be time to blow up the box you're operating in and create a totally new one.

I want to encourage you to create from your own life experiences and intuitive sense regarding where you see that all-important gap in your industry. Again, it's easy to complain about your industry. Instead, I want you to go from complaining about it to committing to fixing it! I want you to intentionally tune in only to your own instinct and intuition and listen to that voice inside you that is almost always right. You will be far more competitive when you stop doing what everyone else does. Revolt against the norms, and you can make millions in the process.

## Celebrate and Elevate Your Mindset

Identifying the gap is only one step. You must produce the solutions that fill that gap. Do so by gaining a better understanding of your prospects' and clients' journeys, experiences, and desires. What are they feeling, and what challenges do they face when they are trying to achieve results in your space? I see too many entrepreneurs concentrating on their competitors rather than their clients! Dedicate your time to falling in love with your clients.

If you don't understand this and, if you fail to see the problems and obstacles from your clients' perspective, you will not be able to create the unique solution they need.

As I said, get yourself in a room (literal or virtual) in which you can interact with entrepreneurs from all different industries and business types. Refuse to stay in a tiny little bubble of people within the same niche as you. There is incredible value in the lessons you can glean from different industries. Even if you are a little fish in a big pond, never assume that other "leaders" in your industry know more than you and are doing a better job. Don't be afraid to follow your instincts and do what you believe. Just because they may be bigger, or have been around longer, doesn't make them right! Do not discount your own expertise. Embrace your passion and intuition. Create based on those alone rather than creating a by-product that results from unconscious bias.

Celebrate and elevate exactly what makes you different and that category of one.

Too many entrepreneurs fail to elevate because they stick to what's already been done and that which they deem is safe and acceptable. I want you to work from imagination and fascination instead. Yes, that involves risk, but it is what opens you up to reaching your maximum potential. Stop worrying about alienating your competitors because you are concerned about sharing your own views. Graduate from that line of thinking. Otherwise, if you run your business based on what everyone else is doing, your achievements and results will never really stand out. You'll be left with average, run-of-the mill, and normal. You'll fit in with the crowd which will ultimately keep you from achieving the kind of greatness and the wealth that comes from creating your own lane.

Stop worrying about being liked, and start focusing all of your energy on making a difference.

## Establishing Your Convictions

- You must revolt against the norms to elevate to where you want to be.

- Have an avatar; know who you are here to serve and exactly what your purpose is.

- Do not niche down too soon or too narrowly; doing so limits your ability to go against industry norms.

- Mixing with other industries helps you eliminate the unconscious bias that often occurs when you surround yourself with similar thinking.

- Do not complain about your industry; commit to fixing what's wrong.

- Concentrate on your clients, not your competitors.

- Never assume other leaders in your industry are right simply because they are bigger or have been around longer.

- Create based on your passion.

# Chapter Eight:

# 5 Essential Steps to Catapult Your Business to a Category of One

*"I often say 'pursue excellence, ignore success.'*
*Success is a by-product of excellence."*
**-Deepak Chopra**

So how do you articulate those things that elevate you above your competitors to gain that coveted category-of-one status and become peerless? Remember that becoming peerless eliminates any potential apples-to-apples comparisons regarding who you are and what you do. Creating an incomparable world-class brand is top priority for the scalability and growth of your business through all economic cycles and market changes. When you focus on being the best at everything you do, you simply and completely eliminate your competition and can move forward with confidence, certainty, and ease. I've said it before, and will say it again: the "extra mile" is never, ever crowded, so that is exactly where you want to place yourself.

As we covered earlier, the first step to standing out is identifying and illuminating your convictions. It's the difference between conviction marketing and the copy-paste, templated approach. I want you to share and illuminate your own deep beliefs about what could (and should) be possible for the future in your industry. What is your compelling vision that will drastically improve the lives of those you're here to serve? In terms of sharing your message, this is what we covered in Chapter 2, going from how-to to hope to true conviction, where you ultimately paint the picture of the future and lead not only by what you say, but by what you do as well. Have the courage to buck the norms, color outside the lines, go against the grain, and zig when everyone else zags.

Step two is where you fill the gap. We've covered this extensively—identifying what is broken or missing in your industry and then creating the change that addresses and fulfills the missing solution. Be more obsessed with your target market than with your product. Concentrate all your energy on solving their problem and enabling them to get results faster. Yes, it may take many months of educating your market about how and why you are different, so commit to the long haul. It is a necessary step to become a "category of one." You disrupt the norms and create an apples-tooranges situation so that prospects cannot lump you in with your competitors. Listen to your gut, develop your intuition, and be the disruptor in your own industry!

Step three involves turning your conviction into a tribe mentality and a global community as we covered in Chapter 5. You take your message to the world and use language that creates a stickiness factor with your followers and engages them to interact with each other as well. Create the special "inner circle" feeling that your prospects and clients truly want. It's all about turning your message into a movement. How many times are you willing to stand on your podium and teach your message and share your conviction? This is exactly what we've done with the *Live Launch Method*. We're enabling entrepreneurs around the globe to change their businesses and their lives every single day. What is your methodology and movement? It's time to gain clarity about that right now. While others focus on minutes and hours, you need to have a "years and decades" focus. This is what visionary leadership is all about. It's not just having an idea but committing to that idea and creating a body of work over a lifetime that supports it. It's commitment to never-ending improvement.

Step four is all about following through. As we covered in Chapter 6, the fortune is in the follow-through. This is the culmination of taking your ideas and convictions to build a world-class program that enables you to make a real and lasting difference. Your flagship program is your message to the market and to the world. It is what allows your clients to achieve superior results. This is where competition actually becomes

> *You must become obsessed with never ending improvement and absolute excellence at what you do.*

a needed component. Competition actually indicates that there is money to be made in your space. When your prospects have experienced subpar service and results from your competitors, you quickly become the obvious choice and the value you provide soars. You must provide superior products, services, and results. This is critical to catapult to category-of-one status.

Finally, step five is all about building a world-class brand. What is a world-class brand and why should you care about it? Unless you focus on creating a superior product, service, or brand, you are placing yourself in the race to the bottom. The opposite of category-of-one status is commoditization; everyone offers it and there is no distinction. The online market has definitely created a lot of commoditization. When you offer a commodity, you will always compete on price, and there will always be little, if any, profit rather than generating real revenue and wealth. Prospects who are drawn to and buy based on price are never loyal and are not worth your time and effort. If you are not obsessed with building a world-class brand, you will be categorized as a commodity, and that is the last place you want to be. There are only two choices: obsession with building the very best product, program, and service, delivering that with excellence, and focusing on never-ending improvement *O R* commoditization and competing on price and facing competitors who are always willing to cut their profits for a sale. Building a world-class brand is the journey of a lifetime, not a daily focus on closing a sale.

To quickly recap:

1. Identify and illuminate your convictions
2. Fill the gap
3. Develop a tribe mentality and build a community
4. Follow through
5. Build a world-class brand

No matter where you are in your business right now, I want you to focus on these five steps. When you do, you can increase your price, blast your profits, and create the coveted category-of-one status!

If you are uncertain about these steps, I encourage you to check out our programs at Kelly Roach Coaching. Your market is not looking for more of the same; they want and need ideas that will change the world. I want to draw your attention to the opportunity that is in front of you while most everyone else is pulling back. At a time when customer service is at an all-time low, with other entrepreneurs cutting back and cutting corners, I want you to examine the situation and determine your opportunity to go "all in" and step into the role of visionary leader that you are destined to become!

## Establishing Your Convictions

- Creating a world-class brand has got to be a top priority for your business.

- Don't settle for short-term wins at the expense of your long-term vision.

- An obsessive focus on being the absolute best option in your market will help you establish brand power that is undeniable.

# Chapter Nine:

# Your Moral Compass Makes Your Marketing Matter

*"When you are able to maintain your own highest standards of integrity—regardless of what others may do—you are destined for greatness."*

**- Napoleon Hill**

K nowing your values and following your own moral compass will make you stand out in your market and serve as a differentiator, setting you apart from your competition.

Let's face it. Anyone can slap together some Facebook ads, an Instagram story, a landing page, and even a course or program. As I've said repeatedly throughout the pages of this book, in the online world today, the barrier to entry is zero. You can be in business in about 30 seconds, trying to replicate what someone else took 15 years to build and suggesting that you are offering the same thing. We all know this.

So what do we do about that, and how do we maintain our sanity within the growing noise of the online space? The idea of having a moral compass simply adds to everything I've shared about conviction marketing and takes it one step further. Allowing your morals to be fully fleshed out in the work you do will undoubtedly help you stand out in a world full of slick marketing and empty promises.

First, caring is the centerpiece of your big breakthrough. In my company, we follow the CARE MORE model, and that has been the number one focus since launching my company. We consider our level of caring more in every decision we make and in every element of the business. The successful results and outcomes our clients get, over and over again, are the direct result of our high-touch, care more model. Our laser focus on client satisfaction, service reviews, auditing, and quality checks show our people that we are committed to making their experience unmatched. Our successful results and outcomes are derived from the success of our clients and how quickly we can help them achieve that success, and caring more allows us to accelerate those results.

When I look at the CARE MORE model, I believe that if you do the right things for the right reasons in your business and focus on simultaneous promotion of all interests—yours, your clients', your company's, and your team's—you will rise to the top. That said, you will very likely need to go through a re-education with your clients as I did with the coaching company. Any time you approach the market with a new idea or concept that seems to be out of alignment with what they've already been conditioned to think, believe, and accept, it may take two to three years to gain real traction and complete buy-in. I went through this very challenge, but I truly believed in what we were doing and why, so I stuck with it, and we're now at the top of our space.

This is definitely a long-game approach. Your prospects have to see the problem, be willing to do something about the problem, and believe that your solution is the right one. That takes time. When you're working on something disruptive and even revolutionary, don't worry that it takes a while to get your message across. You must go through the re-education process with your market. Have patience; it's a multi-year process.

When you apply the CARE MORE model as your centerpiece, it will make your marketing matter. Most companies in the online space fully understand online marketing and do a lot of it, and yes, this marketing can lead to client acquisition. However, there is a difference between successful marketing and running a successful company. The latter requires much more than simply getting clients. You must also retain and re-engage them, get renewals and referrals, ascend them, and increase their lifetime value. If your business is based on an acquisition model, it will lead you to burnout and breakdown and will be impossible to maintain.

If you're wondering how you can do all the things I just mentioned to operate and sustain a successful company, simply doing the right things for the right reason—following your moral compass—will get you there. Here's how we did that inside our coaching company.

## Care More

**C: Cultivating actual relationships.** This is about absolute mastery of your craft. Too many entrepreneurs focus on acquisition, marketing, and brand-building. Those are important but must come *after* you've mastered your craft. You must be the best at what you do and offer a superior product or service. You are meeting people where they are and elevating them through their entire journey. Cultivating actual relationships means understanding that having those one thousand true fans and one hundred ideal clients can create a million-dollar business for you. You carve inroads by creating relationships and caring.

**A: Activate Others' Audiences.** Serve, serve, serve—and serve some more. There are many people who are searching for you. They're in podcast audiences, social media channels, and email lists, but you have to activate them and show up for them. You must make giving back part of your activity every single week. Serve more by delivering to other people's audiences on a variety of platforms. Too many of these potential clients are settling for subpar because they have yet to discover *you*, the person who is going to deliver an innovative solution! Refine your ability to get visible to bring these people into your ecosystem. Focus diligently on providing a superior product or service coupled with incredible customer experience. By doing so, you'll find these prospects not only become clients, they become advocates who'll promote you.

**R: Revolutionize Your Industry.** This is another call to arms. Your industry is looking for you to create that alternate reality we've been discussing, and then they need you to lead them to and through it. Conviction marketing is about seeing the future and being the visionary, and then being willing to commit your life and legacy to it. Be determined to fill the gap. This goes beyond simply seeing what you don't like in your industry and pointing out where things could be different. I want you to commit to disrupting and then leading people in your own lane.

**E: Empower People's Highest Potential.** Focus on your team and your clients and work to help them win and succeed. The goal is to have every person who comes in contact with you become a better person because of the time they spend with you. Work to enable your team and clients to be enriched and fulfilled and feel seen and heard. You must over-deliver to help them create the envisioned future they want and deserve.

Remember: if you make enough people's dreams come true, the same will happen for you!

**M: Movement.** You have to create a movement. You must convert your small group of followers and fans into an audience that listens to your every word and follows your every move. When joining your movement, people should experience superior results, achieve their goals, see their potential, and legitimately have the ability to create the future they want because of your leadership. Your movement includes the tribe language and common beliefs we covered earlier.

**O: Originate Your Own Lane.** Conviction, certainty, and the willingness to dedicate the time to re-educate the market about a new concept that leads to better outcomes puts you in that desired category-of-one lane. There are plenty of leaders and influencers who are in the same space, but they each have a unique nuance, strategy, formula, flavor, and approach—and their own lane. So what's yours? Create your own lane, and don't settle for being second in someone else's. Be the first, best, and only version of you. When you do the right thing for the right reason, your own lane naturally develops.

**R: Renew, Reinvent, Re-engage.** Do this without wavering or diluting your power. People love to follow those who are always learning, always growing, always trying something new. The degree to which you work on yourself sets the bar for your ability to influence others. In following your moral compass, if you want to lead a population and movement, you must commit to your own continuous improvement, renewal, growth, and development. Invest in your own growth as a human being.

**E: Energize.** Is your audience alive with fire, passion, and determination? You must absolutely show up that way for them every single day. They must be inspired by your work ethic, drive, and desire, and be inspired to the degree that they want to replicate it and make their own difference. You want them to aspire to be better because you are making yourself better. Is your own behavior worth replicating? What are you doing to make your followers want to double down on their commitment to you? Consistent action yields conversions. You cannot simply focus on front-end acquisition. You must be committed to what happens after someone places their trust in you. You must continually re-energize yourself and, by doing so, re-energize your audience. The intentionality by which you live dictates your power and ability to unlock more of your potential—what's already inside of you!

Dig deep to really uncover why you are doing what you're doing and why you are on this planet. These principles apply to any business on any platform in any space and in any industry.

> *The culture you create determines the legacy you will perpetuate.*

The CARE MORE model boils down to this: If you care more about getting your clients results, creating a superior product or service, committing to the outcomes your followers achieve, and elevating the experience they have by being around you, then *you are going to rise to the top*. You will be the leader; you will be a category of one; you will be peerless.

The culture you create determines the legacy you will perpetuate. What do you want that legacy to be? If your business decisions and your personal beliefs are in siloes, you must tear down the walls between them. Only then can you actually follow your own moral compass. When you make business decisions based on your personal core values, everything else falls into place. Don't worry about trying to gain instant gratification; you can't. Again, this is a long game, so keep your eye on your dreams and where you want to go. If you employ your moral compass in the way you make every decision, you have an innate and lasting advantage. You will rise to the top. Do the right thing for the right reason, and I assure you, you will achieve your ultimate goal.

## Establishing Your Convictions

- Follow your own moral compass and stand out as a differentiator.

- Caring more should be your centerpiece. It is the key to your big breakthrough.

- Focus on the simultaneous promotion of all stakeholders—your clients, your company, yourself.

- There is a big difference between successful marketing (getting clients) and running a successful company (retaining, getting renewals and referrals, increasing clients' lifetime value)!

- Follow the CARE MORE model:
    - Cultivate actual relationships with the absolute mastery of your craft.
    - Activate others' audiences by serving and giving back every single week.
    - Revolutionize your industry by creating an alternate reality and leading others to and through it.
    - Empower people's highest potential and help them win and succeed.
    - Create a movement in which followers experience superior results and achieve their goals.
    - Originate your own lane and don't settle for being second in someone else's.

- Renew, reinvent, re-engage yourself to make others want to follow you.
- Energize your audience with fire, passion, and determination that is worth replicating.
- The culture you create determines the legacy you will perpetuate.

# Chapter Ten:

# The Millionaire Visionary

*"The only thing worse than being blind is having sight but no vision."*
## - Helen Keller

I n this final chapter, let's really take a good look at how you can live out conviction marketing every day. It's all about connecting your vision and integrity. So what does being a visionary CEO look like?

I've spent a lot of time observing the market in the digital space, monitoring what's working and not working, who's rising (and why), who's falling (and why), along with the trends and evolutions. The conclusion is that conviction marketing is more powerful and more relevant now than ever. I want to be more focused on helping you illuminate your own convictions, so that you can, in turn, serve your clients. The market is craving this positive disruption and needs a well-lit path forward.

First and foremost, as you grow your organization, you have two client groups: those who work for you and those you are being paid to serve. It's important to keep in mind that visionary leaders are servant leaders. Honor those who've linked arms with you to be part of your journey— your team. Also, honor those who trust you for your leadership in building their own organizations and investing in you to show them the way forward.

The majority of your energy as a million-dollar or multi-million-dollar CEO comes down to creating and casting your vision with both your internal clients (your team) and your external clients (those who pay you for your mentorship and leadership). You must spend your energy in both strategic, tangible and intangible ways.

The tangibles are when you lay out your master plan— the big crazy vision you have. It includes the ideas of what you believe the future can look like and bringing into focus that future's impact on the here and now. Too many times, CEOs and entrepreneurs are so fully immersed in, and passionate about, their vision that they presume others know and understand their vision as well as they do. What I want to underscore is that, in casting your vision and making it a million-dollar or multi-million-dollar enterprise, you must make it an integral part of the day-to-day running of your business.

You, as a leader and visionary, are also a salesperson. You are selling your team and clients on your dream, over and over again. To do so, you must paint an incredible picture of your vision. You must communicate your vision and repeatedly share the "what's in it for them" perspective to both your team and clients to gain true buy-in. Conviction marketing isn't just applicable to your go-to market strategy; it's how you get your team fully on board.

A visionary is not simply someone who has big ideas and dreams. Anyone can have those. A true visionary can not only see what's possible, but they have the skill and fortitude to assemble the right group of people around them to implement and execute the steps needed to convert that dream into reality. The visionary coin has two sides. One is the strategy, the idea, seeing something that does not exist today. The other side is where the multi-million-dollar breakthroughs occur. Now you have the dream and vision, but you need people to help implement it. Being a visionary by yourself is not going to get you very far. It truly does take a village.

## Growth Required

As a successful visionary, you must sell your team on the dream, paint an extraordinarily clear picture of the vision, and insert this work into your everyday existence. These three things are the fundamentals that will require you to grow as a leader to ensure you encompass everything needed, not just to be a thinker but to be a creator.

Let's talk about being a visionary in the day-to-day for your market. This has actually been the most powerful lesson for me as an entrepreneur. When you're starting, you likely watch competitors in your industry—those who are doing what you want to do and who are where you want to be—and scan the landscape for successes. At this stage, you are less of a visionary and more of an implementer and executor, taking massive action. In the beginning, you try to follow the rules and the groundwork of those who came before you. And this is the right thing to do because everything must happen in progression. It is the right thing to find a mentor who is doing what you want to do and is doing so successfully. It is the right thing to figure out what does and doesn't work. Focusing on taking massive action is the right thing to do. But...

As you progress through your entrepreneurial journey, the big turning point at which you can step into true visionary leadership is when you effectively disrupt your industry in some way. You cannot achieve that status if you continue to think, act, and make decisions based on what everyone else is doing. This means—and this is such an important part of conviction marketing— that to become a true visionary leader and be what your market craves, you must step into the role of a trusted advisor who teaches things that are not being taught, has conversations that are not being had, and truly looks at the market as a place in which you can serve in a way your prospects and clients have not been served in the past.

I first learned this with my coaching company and quickly learned that to be successful meant breaking away from what everyone else was doing. As I mentioned, this did not occur overnight. It took multiple years of doing the right things for the right reasons... every... single... day.

As a visionary leader, you must be prepared to play an extremely long game. The vast majority of your competitors are looking at things with a very short time frame in mind: *Did it work today? Did I get a return today? Is it impacting sales this week or this month?* I assure you, short-term thinking will never lead you to the levels of success you desire. It will never catapult your business to the next level. You have to be willing to take the time to educate your market and paint the picture of your vision. That takes time—months sometimes, even years. Plan for a long sales cycle, because you are indeed selling.

Think about your own perception of visionary leadership. Do you have a roadmap for how you are going to step into that role? Have you been leading your team with vision every day and in everything you do? Have you been selling your clients on their dreams every single day? Have you been keeping your ideas front and center to drive how you lead and how you show up every day?

When you look at the day-to-day work of visionaries, they spend their time meeting with people and talking about ideas and then working to implement those ideas. They're building things that have never been built before, doing what's never been done before, and choosing faith over fear in pursuit of the ideal outcome for their clients' futures and their own. Yes, it is a long game, every step of the way.

It's in your content, your team meetings, your podcasts and programs, how you build your team and interact with your peers and colleagues. You must let go of the urge to play it safe and instead be willing to move forward in faith over fear to step into the person who is able to persevere to be the visionary. You must commit to getting your message to your market for as long as that takes, regardless of any struggles and setbacks you may face and no matter how hard it seems. This is the essence of visionary leadership.

It's time for some self-assessment. Think through how you have or haven't been leading in your day-to-day activities as a visionary. Everything happens in your mind before it happens in actuality. Let me say that again: everything happens in your mind before it happens in actuality. Decide first to be a visionary; construct the plan of action, and then implement.

This goes hand-in-hand with everything we covered so far in this book. Conviction marketing is all about taking your vision for a much better future and then doing the work to create the well-lit and paved pathway to that future. It's releasing your judgment of others and withholding your opinions about what they're doing, and instead taking complete ownership of what you are creating to fill the gap.

## Establishing Your Convictions

- You have two clients: your team and those you are paid to serve.

- Visionary leaders are first and foremost servant leaders and must serve both internal and external clients.

- As a visionary leader, you are also a salesperson and must sell your team and your clients on your dream by painting a clear and incredible picture of your vision for the future.

- Communicate clearly and define "what's in it for them."

- The visionary coin has two sides: the strategy and idea on one side and the implementation on the other side.

- It's a long game and often takes multiple years of doing the right things for the right reason every single day.

- Move forward with faith over fear.

- Everything happens in your mind before it happens in actuality.

You have the power to change the world and you are being called to step forward to make your dreams come true while helping and serving thousands of others in the process.

Be open to the possibility that inside of you right now is the power, strength, and potential to move mountains and change generations.

I believe in you… and I know you would not have made it to the final pages of this book unless you knew that you have what it takes to be the change, lead the change, and create a movement that changes people's lives forever.

I am your forever fan just because you care enough about the deep and true work that you are called to do in the world to read this book. That means we are already connected and unified in our commitment to be of service, change lives, and achieve our highest potential.

# Now, go create the visionary brand you were meant to build! You've got this!

# About the Author

Kelly Roach transforms overworked entrepreneurs into seven-figure CEOs. With her Executive Fortune 500 experience and results, Kelly combines timeless business principles employed by billion-dollar corporations with the speed and agility of the most powerful online marketing strategies of today.

Kelly's company, Kelly Roach Coaching, is the leading online business education company in North America today. Leveraging scalable intimacy and revolutionizing the way entrepreneurs launch their offers, Kelly's company has catapulted into the multi-millions while helping entrepreneurs around the globe do the same.

In addition to being a best-selling author, Kelly is also an ongoing expert on ABC, NBC, Fox, and The CW. She has been featured in some of the world's leading publications including *Inc.* and *Forbes* and is the host of the Top 50 Marketing podcast, *The Unstoppable Entrepreneur Show*.

Kelly is committed to ongoing philanthropic work, with a 1:1 business model that brings clean drinking water to those who do not have access through her Human Family Foundation.

In addition to running her coaching company with a team of 50+ full-time employees (and growing), Kelly is the co-founder of a second company, Give Her Courage, The Courageous Brand. Kelly founded this company to create a movement designed to give young girls the competitive edge they need to rise to the top, break through barriers, and create lasting change in the world.

Kelly is the co-founder of The Advance Women's Expert Network and the Social Sellers Academy, both of which fill meaningful and powerful gaps in the entrepreneurial space.

**The Kelly Roach Coaching website:**

www.kellyroachcoaching.com

**The Kelly Roach Show:**

www.kellyroachcoaching.com/podcast

**Connect with Kelly:**

**Facebook:** @unstoppableentrepreneurshow

**Facebook Community:** Tribe of Unstoppables

**Instagram:** @Kellyroachofficial

**LinkedIn:** @Kelly Roach

To learn how you can work with Kelly and her team, email Kelly@kellyroachcoaching.com or visit www.kellyroachcoaching.com.